COLORADO WILDLIFE VIEWING GUIDE

Mary Taylor Gray

W9-BAQ-384

FALCON PRESS®

1

ACKNOWLEDGMENTS

Growing public interest in viewing wild animals at home in their natural elements is bringing wildlife management and land conservation organizations together in projects that will enhance Colorado's wildlife legacy. Watchable Wildlife, the sum of their efforts, is dedicated to people who enjoy the thrill of spotting a wild creature and taking home no more than a photograph or a memory.

In Colorado, the program is in its infancy, but each year will bring increased viewing facilities and opportunities. This book is part of that commitment.

The Colorado Wildlife Viewing Guide is a cooperative effort of the agencies who serve as stewards of the state's land and its wild residents, whether their habitats are pristine or surrounded by pavement. This guide is a product of the Colorado Wildlife Heritage Foundation, the Colorado Division of Wildlife, the U.S.D.A. Forest Service, the Bureau of Land Management, the U.S. Fish and Wildlife Service, Defenders of Wildlife, the Bureau of Reclamation, the National Audubon Society, the Colorado Wildlife Federation, Denver Water Department and the Colorado Tourism Board. Valuable assistance also was rendered by the Colorado Chapter of the Wildlife Society and the Boulder County Audubon Society.

Key contributions to site selection and content review also were made by dozens of BLM, Forest Service, and Division of Wildlife field employees, the people who know these special places best. Special thanks also go to Tom Brown, who helped get this viewing guide off the ground.

Equally important were the efforts of the book's steering committee members, who labored through long hours of site selection, organization, production and review. They are: Bob Hernbrode, Melanie Woolever, Lee Upham, Kelly Drake, Hugh Kingery, Lisa Langelier and Andy Love.

Author: Mary Taylor Gray
Project Coordinator: John Gunn
Life Zone Illustrations: Steve Elliott

Front cover photo:
Yellow-bellied marmot. TOM TIETZ

Back cover photos:
Lark bunting. Colorado's state bird. WENDY SHATTIL/BOB ROZINSKI
Great Sand Dunes National Monument. SHERM SPOELSTRA

CONTENTS

3

NORTHEAST REGION

SOUTHEAST REGION

SOUTH CENTRAL REGION

SOUTHWEST REGION

INTRODUCTION

From the broad prairies of the Eastern Plains to the tops of 14,000-foot peaks, Colorado is defined by its wildlife resources. Wildlife is so much a part of our lives that we can take for granted the hawk circling over a prairie dog colony or deer and elk browsing in a meadow. But without the wildlife, Colorado would be infinitely poorer.

Fortunately, wildlife thrives in our state. And we want to help you and your family better enjoy this natural treasure. The National Watchable Wildlife program is designed to provide you with information on enjoying wildlife, be it on a hike, in your backyard or as part of a photo expedition.

In the **Colorado Wildlife Viewing Guide**, we've put together information you'll need to find new places to enjoy a variety of species. And as you enjoy our wildlife, we hope you will also come to better understand and appreciate this great natural heritage and what we need to do today to ensure that our grandchildren will have the same opportunity.

Gary E. Cargill	H. Robert Moore	Perry D. Olson
Regional Forester	State Director	Director
Rocky Mountain Region	Bureau of Land	Colorado Division
U.S.D.A. Forest Service	Management	of Wildlife

PROJECT SPONSORS

The BUREAU OF LAND MANAGEMENT is responsible for the stewardship of 8.3 million acres of public lands in Colorado. The Bureau is committed to managing, protecting, and improving these lands in a manner to serve the needs of the American people. Management is based on the principles of multiple use and sustained yield of our nation's renewable and nonrenewable resources within a framework of environmental responsibility and scientific technology. Most of the BLM-administered lands are located in the western portion of Colorado. The Bureau's Watchable Wildlife program provides the opportunity to view wildlife on these public lands. Bureau of Land Management, Colorado State Office, 2850 Youngfield St., Lakewood, CO 80215. (303) 239-3600.

The BUREAU OF RECLAMATION was created by the Reclamation Act of 1902 to reclaim arid lands in the seventeen western states. Today, the Bureau of Reclamation provides water to more than ten million acres of land. In addition, its multipurpose projects provide municipal and industrial water, hydroelectric power, recreational opportunities, and fish and wildlife enhancement. In Colorado, the Bureau of Reclamation has 365,000 acres of land on which thirty-one dams and reservoirs are located. These reservoirs encompass 50,423 surface acres of water and 516 shoreline miles. Bureau of Reclamation, Denver Office, Denver Federal Center, Denver, CO 80225. (303) 236-9336.

The COLORADO DIVISION OF WILDLIFE's mission is to protect and enhance the wildlife resources of the state and provide an opportunity for people to enjoy them. Wildlife makes a fundamental contribution to the quality of life in Colorado, both aesthetically and economically. Wildlife management is the tool the Division uses to enhance this quality of life. Participation in this publication is part of the Division's ongoing efforts to help people better enjoy wildlife. Colorado Division of Wildlife, 6060 Broadway, Denver, CO 80216. (303) 297-1192.

Watching wildlife is just one of the many outdoor activities enjoyed year round in Colorado. For information on other cultural and recreational opportunities, call the COLORADO TOURISM BOARD, the state's promotional organization, at (800) 433-2656 to request a copy of the Official State Vacation Guide. Other publications such as the Summer Events Guide and state map are also available by calling the toll-free number. Colorado Tourism Board, 1625 Broadway, Suite 1700, Denver, CO 80202. (303) 592-5510.

The COLORADO WILDLIFE HERITAGE FOUNDATION is a nonprofit organization committed to protecting and enhancing Colorado's wildlife resources. The Foundation serves as a repository for land donations, financial gifts and membership dues, and puts them to work to assure that Colorado's wildlife thrives. Special attention will be paid to Colorado's nongame and endangered wildlife. Colorado Wildlife Heritage Foundation, P.O. Box 211512, Denver, CO 80221. (303) 291-7212.

DENVER WATER is the caretaker and provider of water for almost one million people in the Denver metropolitan area. Through wise management of watersheds and reservoirs, Denver Water balances its customers' interests in both high-quality drinking water and a beautiful, healthy Colorado. Denver Water, 1600 W. 12th Ave., Denver, CO 80254. (303) 628-6000.

The U.S.D.A. FOREST SERVICE manages 16 million acres of wildlife habitat in Colorado under a mandate to protect, improve and wisely use the nation's natural resources for multiple purposes. The seven national forests and two national grasslands in Colorado are sponsors of this program to promote the fish and wildlife on national forest service lands. For further information on national forest opportunities in Colorado, contact: U.S.D.A. Forest Service, 11177 W. 8th Ave., Lakewood, CO 80225. (303) 236-9431.

The U.S. FISH AND WILDLIFE SERVICE administers 77,179 acres in Colorado, including four wildlife refuges, the Rocky Mountain Arsenal, and two fish hatcheries. Its mission is to conserve, protect and enhance the nation's fish and wildlife and their habitats for the benefit of the American people. Major responsibilities include migratory birds, endangered species and inland fisheries management. U.S. Fish and Wildlife Service, P.O. Box 25486, Denver Federal Center, Denver, CO 80225. (303) 236-7904.

DEFENDERS OF WILDLIFE is a national, nonprofit organization of more than 80,000 members and supporters dedicated to preserving the natural abundance and diversity of wildlife and its habitat. A one-year membership is $20 and includes six issues of the bimonthly magazine *Defenders*. To join or for further information, write or call Defenders of Wildlife, 1244 Nineteenth Street, N.W., Washington, DC 20036. (202) 659-9510.

MAP INFORMATION

Colorado is divided into six travel regions shown on this map. Wildlife viewing sites are numbered consecutively in general patterns from west to east or north to south. Each region in this book forms a seperate section in this book, and each section begins with a detailed map of that region. Directions to each viewing site appear on small maps adjacent to each site description. Key features of the site maps appear on the legend below:

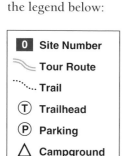

0	**Site Number**
〰	**Tour Route**
⋯	**Trail**
Ⓣ	**Trailhead**
Ⓟ	**Parking**
△	**Campground**

FEATURED WILDLIFE

Songbirds   Upland Birds   Waterfowl

Wading Birds   Shorebirds   Marine Birds

Birds of Prey   Small Mammals   Hoofed Mammals

Carnivores   Freshwater Mammals   Fish

Reptiles/Amphibians   Insects   Wildflowers

5
1
2   **4**
6
3   MAYBELL ○   ○   **7**
8   CRAIG
○ DINOSAUR
9 ○   **NW**
MEEKER
14
○
⑦⓪   GLENWOOD
SPRINGS
10 GRAND
JUNCTION   **13**   ASPEN ○
11 ○
DELTA
12   ○   **96** **95**
99   **98** ○
MONTROSE   GUNNISON
SW   **100**   LAKE
CITY
TELLURIDE   **101** ○
103 ○
85
○ DOVE CREEK   **102**
105
104
107
○   **108**   PAGOSA
CORTEZ **106**   ○ **109**   **110** SPRINGS
DURANGO   ○

FACILITIES AND RECREATION

Parking   Restrooms   Picnic   Trails   Handicap Accessible   Entry Fee   Cross-Country Skiing

Small Boats   Restaurant   Boat Ramp   Camping   Lodging   Bicycling

SITE OWNER/MANAGER ABBREVIATIONS

BLM - Bureau of Land Management
BOR - Bureau of Reclamation
CDOW - Colorado Division of Wildlife
CDPOR - Colorado Division of Parks
    and Outdoor Recreation

NPS - National Park Service
PVT - Private ownership
USFS - U.S. Forest Service
USFWS - U.S. Fish and
    Wildlife Service

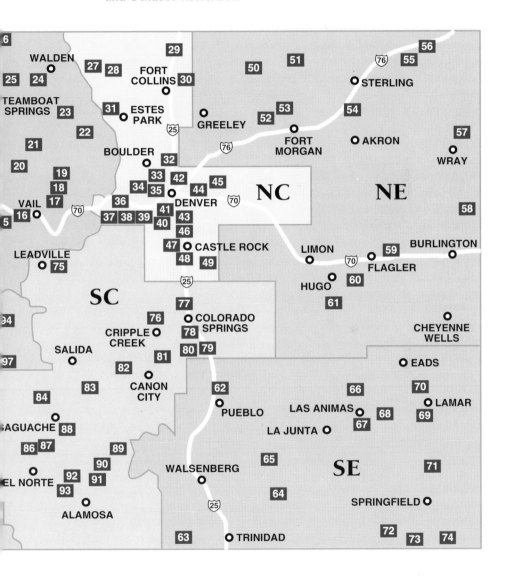

Do Something Wild . . .
Share With Wildlife

DO SOMETHING WILD. . . SHARE WITH WILDLIFE

Here's how you can help wildlife in Colorado. Make a tax-deductible contribution through your state income tax form; or mail a direct tax-deductible contribution to the Nongame Fund at the Colorado Division of Wildlife.

HOW TO USE THIS GUIDE

The wildlife viewing sites in this guide are grouped according to the state's six travel regions used by the Colorado Tourism Board.

Each site description includes the featured wildlife and the habitat in which species may be seen. Notes of precaution relating to road conditions, safety, viewing limitations and land ownership restrictions are included. Site descriptions also display icons for featured wildlife, available facilities, site owner/manager initials, and when applicable, a telephone number where additional site information may be obtained. Each viewing site ultimately will be marked by the binoculars logo, symbolic of the wildlife viewing opportunities found across the nation.

VIEWING HINTS

•The first and last hours of the day are generally the best times to view or photograph most animals. Wildlife viewing is usually poor during the middle of the day, especially during Colorado's relatively infrequent hot spells.

•Be quiet. Quick movements and loud noises will normally scare wildlife. Your car can act as an effective "blind," allowing you to watch animals without alarming them. Whenever cover is unavailable, sit quietly, act disinterested and gaze all around, being careful never to stare directly at the animals.

•Binoculars, spotting scopes, and telephoto camera lenses will help you to get that close-up look. You are probably too close if the animals alter their behavior, stop feeding, or appear nervous. If you note these signs, sit quietly or move away slowly until they resume their original behavior.

•Be patient. Wait quietly for animals to enter or return to an area. Give yourself plenty of time to allow animals to move within your view. Patience is often rewarded with a more complete viewing experience.

•For a safer and more complete viewing experience, supplement this guide with a good road atlas and field guides to western plants and animals.

OUTDOOR ETHICS

•Honor the rights of private landowners and gain permission before entering their property.

•Respect the rights of other wildlife viewers. Approaching animals too closely, making loud noises, and sudden movement are inappropriate.

•Neither man nor pets should ever chase wildlife, and harassment of wild animals is unlawful. Pets are best left at home or in the car during wildlife viewing excursions.

•Wild baby animals look cute and helpless, but resist the urge to handle the young creatures. They usually have not been orphaned or abandoned, and their parents are often nearby.

•Honor your own right to enjoy the outdoors in the future. Leave wildlife habitat in better condition than you found it. Pick up litter that you encounter and dispose of it properly.

COLORADO'S LIFE ZONES

With elevations ranging from 3,350 feet to 14,443 feet above sea level, Colorado has a diversity of plant and animal communities called *life zones*.

URBAN

Urban areas, which occur at a variety of altitudes throughout the state, carry a mix of native and introduced vegetation. Many animals in these areas have adapted to life close to humans, so surprisingly good wildlife viewing can be found in parks, open spaces, greenbelts along waterways, and even in and around manmade structures.

GRASSLAND

The prairie grassland found east of the mountains is semi-arid. It's a land of perennial grasses, shrubs, and forbs, with trees found along waterways. About 40% of Colorado was once grassland. Now, most grassland is in agricultural use.

RIPARIAN

Riparian habitats (wetlands) are found along rivers, streams, ponds, and water sources from the plains to the alpine tundra. They include cattail marshes, streamside cottonwood groves, willow thickets, and much more. Nearly 75% of wildlife depends, to some degree, on wetlands.

MONTANE SHRUBLANDS

This transition zone of the Front Range foothills links the grasslands to the mountains. It is open country of Gambel oak and mountain mahogany.

MONTANE FORESTS

This zone is dominated by ponderosa pine on dry, south-facing slopes and Douglas-fir on moist, cooler, north-facing slopes. Aspen grow in areas of fire, avalanche, or other previous disturbance.

SEMI-DESERT SHRUBLANDS

Found primarily on Colorado's Western Slope, this arid, rough country of dry washes and low shrubs is dominated by big sagebrush.

PINYON PINE/JUNIPER WOODLANDS

This is open, rolling, semi-arid country with extensive woodlands of pinyon pine and juniper. Between these wooded stands are open areas of grasses, shrubs, and forbs.

SUBALPINE FOREST

These thick, moist forests of subalpine fir and Engelmann spruce, where deep snow persists into summer, extend to timberline. Lodgepole pine and aspen grow at lower edges, with gnarled limber and bristlecone pines in upper areas and along exposed ridges.

ALPINE TUNDRA

The tundra is a treeless land of low-growing shrubs and plants punctuated by boulderfields, rock gardens, and talus slopes. The harsh nature of life at this altitude is belied each summer by the spectacular blooming of alpine wildflowers.

NORTHWEST REGION

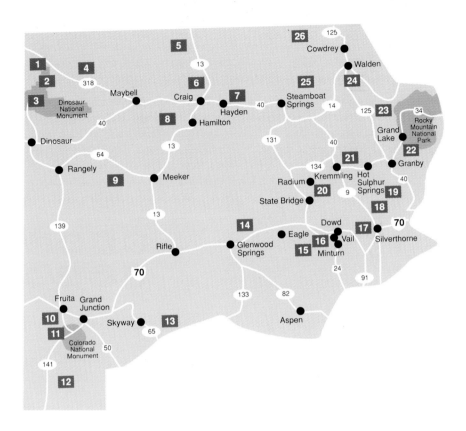

SITE 1 BROWNS PARK NATIONAL WILDLIFE REFUGE	**SITE 15** YEOMAN PARK
SITE 2 GATES OF LODORE	**SITE 16** DOWD JUNCTION ELK VIEWING AREA
SITE 3 HARPERS CORNER ROAD/ECHO PARK	**SITE 17** ALFRED M. BAILEY BIRD NESTING AREA
SITE 4 SAND WASH BASIN	**SITE 18** BLUE RIVER STATE WILDLIFE AREA
SITE 5 SAGE GROUSE LEKS	
SITE 6 CEDAR MOUNTAIN	**SITE 19** SUGARLOAF CAMPGROUND BOARDWALK
SITE 7 MORGAN BOTTOMS	
SITE 8 AXIAL BASIN	**SITE 20** TROUGH ROAD
SITE 9 RIO BLANCO STATE WILDLIFE AREA	**SITE 21** KREMMLING PRONGHORN VIEWING SITE
SITE 10 HORSETHIEF CANYON STATE WILDLIFE AREA	**SITE 22** PINE BEACH
	SITE 23 ILLINOIS RIVER MOOSE VIEWING SITE
SITE 11 COLORADO NATIONAL MONUMENT	**SITE 24** ARAPAHO NATIONAL WILDLIFE REFUGE
SITE 12 TELEPHONE TRAIL	
SITE 13 CRAG CREST TRAIL	**SITE 25** HIDDEN AND TEAL LAKES
SITE 14 HANGING LAKE	**SITE 26** BIG CREEK LAKES

1 BROWNS PARK NATIONAL WILDLIFE REFUGE

Description: A series of ponds and wet meadows along the Green River managed for waterfowl, featuring steep rocky slopes, alluvial benches, and bottomlands along the river. Check at the visitor center for specific viewing opportunities.

Viewing Information: Prime area for waterfowl viewing. Canada geese, mallards, redheads, canvasbacks, green-winged and cinnamon teal, ruddy ducks, common mergansers, and other ducks use the refuge. Other birds include coots, great blue herons, three grebe species, white-faced ibis, sandhill cranes, common loons, common snipe, Wilson's phalaropes, several sandpipers, dowitchers, kingfishers, golden and bald eagles, hummingbirds, swallows, and other songbirds. The bird checklist includes 199 species. Watch for mule deer, coyotes, beavers, muskrats, and prairie dogs.

Ownership: USFWS (303-365-3613)
Size: 13,455 acres
Closest Town: Maybell
Directions: See map below

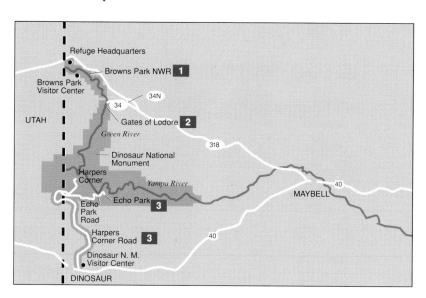

Trees, thickets, and waterways make particularly good viewing areas because they provide cover, food and nesting sites.

2 GATES OF LODORE

Description: Within the northern portion of Dinosaur National Monument stands the striking portal into the Canyon of Lodore on the Green River. Boxelder/cottonwood riparian habitat along the river, canyon walls and benches typified by sagebrush, and pinyon/juniper woodlands with Douglas-fir in moist areas. A one-mile nature trail begins at the campground. Check at the visitor center for information on the site and boating permits.

Viewing Information: Lots of migrant waterfowl, including scaup, mallards, pintails, and wigeons. Good chance to see raptors, including golden eagles at the campground, occasional peregrine and prairie falcons, as well as sharp-shinned, Cooper's, rough-legged, ferruginous, and red-tailed hawks, and kestrels in the canyon. Watch for gnatcatchers, kingbirds, flycatchers, warblers, and other songbirds, plus numerous brush and grassland songbirds. Side-blotched and eastern fence lizards are common in rocky areas.

Ownership: NPS (303-374-2216)
Size: Sixty acres
Closest Town: Maybell
Directions: See map opposite page

3 HARPERS CORNER ROAD/ECHO PARK

Description: A self-guided tour from the Dinosaur National Monument visitor center to Echo Park. Echo Park is a sandy beach area at the junction of the Yampa and Green rivers beneath magnificent sandstone cliffs. Drier slopes and benches typified by sagebrush and pinyon/juniper woodlands, with Douglas-fir and Boxelder/willow communities along the river. Check first at the visitor center for information and road conditions into Echo Park. Boating permit required.

Viewing Information: Mule deer are usually visible from the road; occasional elk and bighorn sheep. Waterfowl, some shorebirds, and possibly river otter or beaver are seen along the Green and Yampa rivers; songbirds in riparian zones. Good raptor watching—with golden eagles, red-tailed and ferruginous hawks, kestrels, and prairie falcons common. Goshawks, Cooper's and sharp-shinned hawks occasionally seen. Watch for peregrine falcons around cliff areas in Echo Park. Cliffs are closed to climbing in spring and summer due to nesting. Watch cliff overhangs for swallows, and canyon and rock wrens.

Ownership: NPS (303-374-2216)
Size: Forty-mile drive
Closest Town: Dinosaur
Directions: See map opposite page

4 SAND WASH BASIN

Description: A large, arid basin typified by sagebrush and salt desert shrubs, ringed by juniper-covered hills. The basin rim is characterized by rocky sandstone outcrops. A series of drainages runs through the basin, but they are dry most of the year. Vermillion Bluffs on the northwest edge of the rim is a badlands-like area. The arid basin offers dramatic, scenic terrain. County roads are passable by passenger car only in dry weather.

Viewing Information: The large, sagebrush basin is good winter range for pronghorn. Golden eagles are often seen hunting over the basin; they roost and nest along the rim. Burrowing owls inhabit prairie dog towns April through August. Great horned owls are common. With few trees in the area, they roost in cavities in the banks of washes and drainages. Other raptors include ferruginous and red-tailed hawks and prairie falcons.

Ownership: BLM (303-824-4441)
Size: 100,000 acres
Closest Town: Maybell
Directions: See map this page

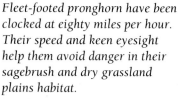

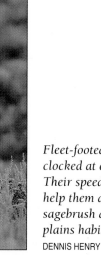

Fleet-footed pronghorn have been clocked at eighty miles per hour. Their speed and keen eyesight help them avoid danger in their sagebrush and dry grassland plains habitat.

DENNIS HENRY

Description: Leks, or breeding grounds, are open, elevated areas in sagebrush country. Sage grouse require sagebrush habitat in large quantities. Because leks are difficult to locate in the dark, search out your viewing site in the afternoon so you can find it again before daylight.

Viewing Information: From mid-March through late May, male sage grouse perform a ritualized courtship dance on ancestral leks, or dancing grounds. They strut around and make a resonant popping or hooting by inflating their large throat sacs. Best viewing time is just before dawn. Your car can act as a blind so the birds accept viewers. Stay on roads and trails and don't leave your car while any birds are on the lek or they will flush.

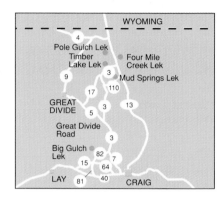

Ownership: PVT, BLM (303-824-4441)
Size: N/A
Closest Town: Craig
Directions: See map this page

A male sage grouse dances on a lek—or strutting ground—to attract mates during the spring breeding season. Take care not to disturb these early-morning dancing displays when viewing them. MICHAEL S. SAMPLE

25

6 CEDAR MOUNTAIN

Description: A mountain shrub community of sagebrush, serviceberry, and snowberry with scattered pinyon/juniper woodlands. A cliff area offers nesting habitat for raptors. An interpretive trail is planned.

Viewing Information: Golden eagles can be observed soaring and hunting, but keep away from the cliff face early March through early July during nesting. Watch for turkey vultures soaring on the thermals. Small mammals you may see include white-tailed jackrabbits, cottontails, and Wyoming ground squirrels. Excellent viewing of shrubland songbirds, with lots of towhees, flycatchers, warblers, and pinyon jays. Mule deer use the area, and elk are seen during spring and fall migration. Pronghorn are sometimes visible on the drive to the mountain. Watch for bald eagles year-round along the Yampa River near Craig.

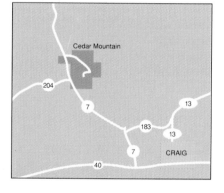

Ownership: BLM (303-824-4441)
Size: 800 acres
Closest Town: Craig
Directions: See map this page

The magnificent golden eagle is one of the West's largest birds of prey. Mature golden eagles are distinguished by golden feathers on the nape of the head and neck.

W. PERRY CONWAY

Description: The Bottoms is flat to rolling country of grazing land and grain fields, with cottonwood riparian habitat along the Yampa River. Foothills terrain surrounds the valley bottom. Noncultivated land is typified by sagebrush, chokecherry, and serviceberry. Land is private so viewing is from the road.

Viewing Information: Morgan Bottoms is a spring and fall staging area for migrating sandhill cranes. Watch for them flying overhead or feeding during the day in grain fields; in spring the cranes can be seen dancing and jumping. Largest concentrations occur in fall, when as many as 1,000 cranes gather. In spring, sage grouse are visible at dawn and dusk, performing on a lek along County Road 80. For organized spring viewing trips to see sage, blue, and sharp-tailed grouse on private land, contact the CDOW in Craig.

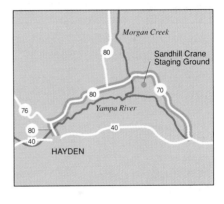

Ownership: PVT (303-824-3046)
Size: Ten-mile drive
Closest Town: Hayden
Directions: See map this page

The male sandhill crane begins his courtship ritual with a leap into the air. The spring dance in open fields occurs prior to the cranes' relocation to nesting areas elsewhere.

WENDY SHATTIL/BOB ROZINSKI

27

8 AXIAL BASIN

Description: A series of rolling, sagebrush-covered ridges and drainages provides important winter range for deer and elk and year-long habitat for pronghorn. Check road conditions prior to winter visits. A seventy-mile loop can be made from Craig with excellent viewing of big game animals along County Road 17 in Axial Basin.

Viewing Information: Elk, mule deer, and pronghorn easily visible from the road. Watch for bald eagles where the highway crosses the Yampa River. Golden eagles and rough-legged hawks also winter in the basin. Keep an eye out for sage grouse. Small mammals include jackrabbits and cottontails, and occasional weasels and coyotes. Watch for winter grassland birds such as horned larks. Best viewing December to March.

Ownership: BLM (303-824-4441)
Size: Twenty-mile drive
Closest Town: Craig
Directions: See map this page

The cottontail—an adaptable, abundant, and often-seen Colorado resident—is found in brushy foothills terrain.
CLAUDE STEELMAN

28

9 RIO BLANCO LAKE STATE WILDLIFE AREA

Description: Upland areas around the reservoir are greasewood shrubland and grassland. Willow/hawthorn bottoms along the river, with a small mixed stand of cottonwood and juniper. Wet meadows of cattail and bulrush, with tamarisk and saltgrass around old river oxbows. Approximately six miles upriver from Meeker, watch for BLM's fifty-five-acre Beefsteak Gulch riparian site with a pulloff on the south side of the highway.

Viewing Information: Rio Blanco is a stopover point for migrating waterfowl and shorebirds, especially in spring. Watch for marbled godwits, avocets, phalaropes, dowitchers, willets, yellowlegs; cattle egrets, and occasional snowy and American egrets; also gulls, terns, and grebes. There is a great blue heronry in the cottonwoods just off the southwest boundary; good viewing from the road along the canal. Keep an eye out for loons, ospreys, swans, cranes, white pelicans, and diving ducks in spring and fall. Wintering bald eagles and rough-legged hawks are common along the White River. Many marsh and riparian songbirds in willow bottoms, and beaver are active along the river.

Ownership: BLM, CDOW (303-878-4493)
Size: 500 acres
Closest Town: Meeker
Directions: See map below

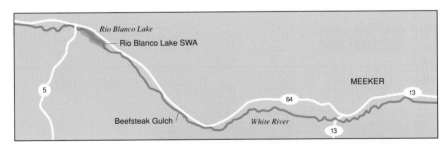

Great blue herons nest in heronries, colonies typically located in cottonwood groves. The large, long-legged anglers can commonly be seen near water.
W. Perry Conway

10 HORSETHIEF CANYON STATE WILDLIFE AREA

Description: This state wildlife area encompasses cottonwood riparian zones along the Colorado River. Horsethief is a transition zone of irrigated agricultural fields and wildlife feeding plots. The terrain rises into shrubby canyonlands of red sandstone rock formations and cliff faces, with scattered pinyon/juniper woodlands.

Viewing Information: Desert bighorn sheep are occasionally seen in rocky areas. Mule deer inhabit the area year-round, with greater concentrations in fall as they move into the fields to feed. Good waterfowl viewing along the river, especially in fall, including Canada geese, mallards, and other dabbling ducks, and some wood ducks. Great blue herons use the area in summer; bald eagles are very visible along the river in winter. Watch also for golden eagles, peregrine falcons, and grassland raptors such as red-tailed and Swainson's hawks. A variety of songbirds uses the riparian habitat along the river in spring and summer. Though not easily viewed, there are four species of endangered native fish in the Colorado River—Colorado squawfish, bonytail and humpback chub, and razorback sucker.

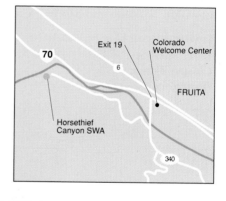

Ownership: CDOW (303-248-7175)
Size: 1,050 acres
Closest Town: Fruita
Directions: See map this page

Mallards are called dabblers because they dip into shallow water to feed on submerged plants.
KEN ARCHER

The bald eagle, America's national symbol, gains its distinctive white head and tail plumage by age five. Hundreds of bald eagles winter in Colorado, but nesting pairs are uncommon. D. ROBERT FRANZ

11 COLORADO NATIONAL MONUMENT

Description: An outstanding scenic area of red sandstone canyons and rock formations along the northern tip of the Uncompahgre Plateau overlooking the Grand Valley. Pinyon/juniper forested mesas with some grassy areas, Gambel oak, sagebrush, and relic stands of Douglas-fir. Some cottonwoods, willows, and tamarisk grow along seasonal streams in the canyon bottoms. Inquire at the visitor center for specific viewing opportunities.

Viewing Information: Golden eagles and red-tailed hawks visible year-round, with turkey vultures April to September. Watch for bald eagles in winter along the Colorado River outside the monument. Active peregrine falcon aerie; watch for the adults hunting around cliffs. Scrub and pinyon jays, Gambel's quail, doves, magpies, canyon wrens, violet-green swallows, and white-throated swifts are all common. A variety of other songbirds may be seen. Mule deer are visible in winter around the visitor center, with occasional elk. Desert bighorn sheep inhabit Kodels Canyon, which requires a back-country hike. Watch for tracks and sign of mountain lions. Good reptile viewing in sunny, rocky areas, with collared, side-blotched, sagebrush, and eastern fence lizards; whiptails; and bullsnakes all common.

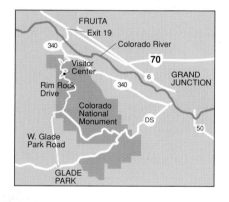

Ownership: NPS (303-858-3617)
Size: 20,450 acres
Closest Town: Grand Junction/Fruita
Directions: See map this page

The collared lizard is easily recognized by its yellow and black neck collar. The reptile also is characterized by its pushup-like bobbing motion. This lizard basks on warm, rocky outcroppings in southern Colorado.
SHERM SPOELSTRA

Description: Mixed community of old-growth aspen and ponderosa pine. The trail passes through the forest to the rim of Carson Hole, where you can look into the canyon bottom to see willow riparian areas, wetlands, and beaver ponds along La Fair Creek. Trails lead along the rim and descend to the canyon floor through mixed conifer forest.

Viewing Information: Area of intense use by cavity nesting birds, offering a variety of species due to the age and diversity of the tree community. Nesting species include flammulated and pygmy owls, flickers, hairy woodpeckers, red-naped and Williamson's sapsuckers, mountain chickadees, pygmy and white-breasted nuthatches, violet-green swallows, and western bluebirds. A variety of raptors use the area such as red-tailed, Cooper's, and sharp-shinned hawks, also kestrels and goshawks. Watch also for flycatchers, poorwills, vireos, towhees, juncos, warblers, and many other songbirds. Active beaver colony along the creek.

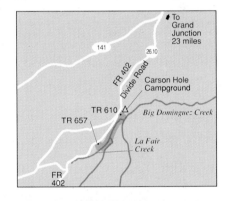

Ownership: USFS (303-242-8211)
Size: Three-mile trail
Closest Town: Grand Junction
Directions: See map this page

The flicker depends on tree cavities for nesting. Found throughout Colorado, flickers in flight are recognized by their white rump patch and undulating flying motion.
HARRY ENGELS

33

13 CRAG CREST TRAIL

Description: This national recreation trail follows the backbone of the Grand Mesa along a ridge rising 300 feet above the mesa plateau. Elevations along the trail range from 10,150 to 11,189 feet, the highest point on the mesa. This is a great geological site. Rocky cliffs drop off on both sides, with lakes visible at the bottom. Outstanding panoramic vistas of the entire mesa. Primarily subalpine forest of spruce/fir and aspen, with open meadows. The trail is steep and rocky in places. Species checklist and brochure available at the visitor center at Cobbett Lake.

Viewing Information: Golden eagles use the cliffs, and the rocky ridge is a raptor migration site. Good site to hear fall elk bugling. Lots of mule deer browse in meadows and around lake edges. Watch for pikas and marmots in rocky areas. Other mammals include chickarees, chipmunks, snowshoe hares, and porcupines. Many birds can be seen—ravens, woodpeckers, chickadees, hummingbirds, and blue grouse.

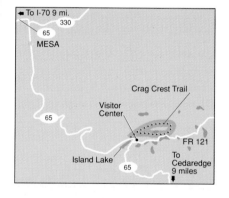

Ownership: USFS (303-242-8211)
Size: Ten-mile loop trail
Closest Town: Cedaredge
Directions: See map this page

Pikas spend the short summers gathering huge quantities of food and storing it away for the long winter. Their sharp whistle is a familiar sound in the Colorado high country. TOM TIETZ

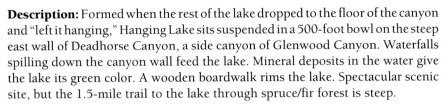

14 HANGING LAKE

Description: Formed when the rest of the lake dropped to the floor of the canyon and "left it hanging," Hanging Lake sits suspended in a 500-foot bowl on the steep east wall of Deadhorse Canyon, a side canyon of Glenwood Canyon. Waterfalls spilling down the canyon wall feed the lake. Mineral deposits in the water give the lake its green color. A wooden boardwalk rims the lake. Spectacular scenic site, but the 1.5-mile trail to the lake through spruce/fir forest is steep.

Viewing Information: Watch for black and white-throated swifts feeding above the lake. The black swifts nest behind the waterfalls. Best place to watch birds is from the boardwalk. Good trout viewing from the boardwalk into the clear water. Watch for other montane wildlife such as Clark's nutcrackers, gray jays, tree and violet-green swallows, chipmunks, and golden-mantled ground squirrels.

Ownership: USFS (303-328-6388)
Size: Fifteen acres
Closest Town: Glenwood Springs
Directions: See map this page

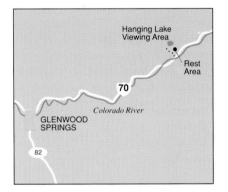

Hanging Lake is easily accessible from a parking lot off Interstate-70. The lake east of Glenwood Springs offers scenic beauty and abundant wildlife. DAN PEHA

15 YEOMAN PARK

Description: Glacial valley surrounded by slopes of subalpine forest, with sagebrush on lower slopes. Extensive wet meadows along East Brush Creek. Thick spruce/fir forests cover the north-facing slopes, with aspen on the south-facing slope. Extensive recreational opportunities include camping, fishing, hunting, mountain biking, and cross-country skiing.

Viewing Information: An extensive beaver colony at the upper end of the valley offers good evening viewing, sometimes with two to three colonies active. Best viewed from the south side just below Fulford Cave Road (Forest Road 418). Good opportunity to see brook and rainbow trout in very clear pools. Elk wintering range. Watch for small mammals such as chickarees, marmots, and rock and golden-mantled ground squirrels. You may see signs of coyotes, weasels, and bears. Northern harriers and Swainson's and red-tailed hawks common. Keep an eye out for woodland hawks like Cooper's, sharp-shinned, and goshawks. Some waterbirds can be seen—mainly sandpipers in wet meadows, mallards, and an occasional merganser.

Ownership: USFS (303-328-6388)
Size: 1,000 acres
Closest Town: Eagle
Directions: See map this page

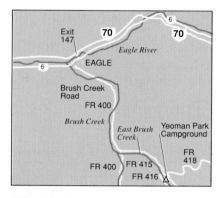

Nature's engineer, the beaver, plays a habitat construction role important to other species. Beaver dams form ponds that become home to fish, mammals, and birds.

DENNIS HENRY

Description: Steep, southwest-facing slopes covered with mountain shrubs—mountain mahogany, chokecherry, and serviceberry—and small stands of aspen and lodgepole pine. The Eagle River runs along the base.

Viewing Information: Winter range for several hundred elk. Good viewing from U.S. 24. The animals are found in draws during the day, moving to open slopes to feed in morning and evening. A viewing area is being built at the Holy Cross Ranger District office.

Ownership: USFS (303-827-5715)
Size: 1,000 acres
Closest Town: Minturn
Directions: See map this page

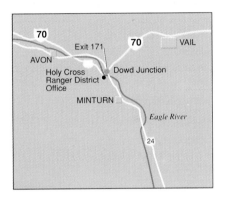

This bull is "bugling"— a high-pitched sound which is part of the glamorous species' fall mating ritual. Colorado has the largest population of elk in the United States.

DENNIS HENRY

17 ALFRED M. BAILEY BIRD NESTING AREA

Description: Willow-dominated wet meadow in a valley surrounded by slopes of spruce/fir and aspen. The trail from the parking lot passes through lodgepole pine forest. The site is located in the Eagles Nest Wilderness Area and is an active study area. Please observe all wilderness rules and respect any research being done.

Viewing Information: The convergence of a multitude of habitats makes this a prime site for bird watching. Forty-three breeding species have been documented. Watch for pine siskins, red-naped and Williamson's sapsuckers, broad-tailed and rufous hummingbirds, Wilson's, MacGillivray's, and yellow-rumped warblers, and a variety of flycatchers, finches, sparrows, and other songbirds. To view bird banding, and possibly help out, contact the Colorado Bird Observatory, (303) 659-4348.

Ownership: USFS (303-468-5400)
Size: 640 acres
Closest Town: Silverthorne
Directions: See map this page

18 BLUE RIVER STATE WILDLIFE AREA

Description: Three parcels of mountain riparian habitat along the Blue River and its tributary creeks, surrounded by sagebrush uplands, irrigated hay meadows, and forested slopes of aspen and mixed conifers.

Viewing Information: Numerous songbirds along the river. Watch for dippers and goldeneyes along the water in winter, and warblers among the willows in summer. Great blue herons and sandpipers are occasionally sighted. Other waterfowl include mallards, teal, and Canada geese. Golden eagles are sometimes seen in summer, bald eagles in winter. Other raptors include kestrels, red-tailed hawks, and an occasional prairie falcon. Weasels, raccoons, and foxes use the area. A .5-mile nature trail with interpretive signs is planned.

Ownership: CDOW (303-725-3557)
Size: 111 acres
Closest Town: Silverthorne
Directions: See map above

Description: The 2,500-foot-long boardwalk crosses the Williams Fork River through a series of beaver ponds and marshy wetlands, and passes through a combination of lodgepole pine forest, aspen stands, and alder/willow bottoms. Lateral boardwalks, three viewing decks built over the stream, and several seating areas facilitate viewing at the beaver ponds. The entire boardwalk and the trail to the campground are wheelchair-accessible. Interpretive signs are being developed.

Viewing Information: Great access to mountain riparian area. Lots of beaver activity. Beaver viewing at dawn and dusk—dams, lodges, and other signs are very visible. Boardwalk over pools allows good views of brook and rainbow trout. Watch for squirrels, rabbits, chipmunks, and other small mammals in the campground. Deer and elk occasionally visible. Hummingbirds, warblers, and other songbirds are seen among the willows, and dippers and spotted sandpipers along the river.

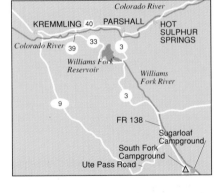

Ownership: USFS (303-724-4004)
Size: 360 acres
Closest Town: Parshall
Directions: See map this page

Brook trout, not native to Colorado, are popular with sportsmen. "Brookies" favor smaller coldwater streams. KEN ARCHER

20 | TROUGH ROAD

Description: Twenty-eight mile drive from Kremmling to State Bridge along the Colorado River. The route climbs open sagebrush hillsides before descending through mixed conifer woodlands, with aspen on higher parts and cottonwood groves on the valley floor. Dirt road is suitable for passenger cars in dry weather.

Viewing Information: Prime wintertime viewing of mule deer and elk. The route passes Radium State Wildlife Area, considered some of the finest deer winter range in the state. Watch for bald eagles along the river December to April. Other raptors may be seen in open areas, with jays and mountain chickadees in wooded areas. Swainson's hawks, turkey vultures, mountain bluebirds, red-naped sapsuckers, and tree and violet-green swallows are summer residents.

Ownership: BLM, PVT, CDOW (303-724-3437)
Size: Twenty-eight-mile drive
Closest Town: Kremmling
Directions: See map this page

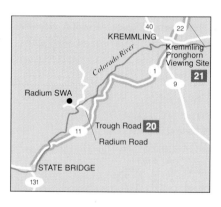

21 | KREMMLING PRONGHORN VIEWING SITE

Description: Excellent pronghorn viewing in rolling, open sagebrush habitat. Stay on the county road while viewing because the animals are on private land.

Viewing Information: Pronghorn inhabit the area year round. Large groups begin to assemble in late summer. Watch for animals on the east side of County Road 22 just north of Kremmling.

Ownership: PVT (303-725-3557)
Size: Two miles of road
Closest Town: Kremmling
Directions: See map above

Description: This picnic site along the shore of Shadow Mountain Lake is surrounded by lodgepole pine forest coming down to the water's edge, with cattail/sedge wetlands along the water's edge. Several offshore islands are accessible by canoe. Observe the seasonal closure signs and avoid those islands where osprey are nesting. Additional bald eagle viewing opportunities at nearby Double A Bar Ranch. Contact the USFS district office at for further information and dates of seasonal closures.

Viewing Information: Watch for ospreys hunting on the reservoir from May to September. You may observe their nests on offshore islands with binoculars. Bald eagles are often seen in winter. Excellent beaver viewing at dusk from June through September; watch for them swimming in the channels between the islands and shore. A beaver lodge directly east of the wetlands is very visible with binoculars. Otters may be seen in the water or along the shore at dusk. Excellent waterfowl viewing includes nesting Canada geese, mallards, wood ducks, and mergansers. Migrants include goldeneyes, scaups, buffleheads, ruddy ducks, green and blue-winged teal, pintails, and other dabbling ducks, grebes, and loons.

Ownership: USFS (303-887-3331)
Size: Ten acres
Closest Town: Grand Lake
Directions: See map this page

Scattered crayfish skeletons and fishy odors indicate the presence of the river otter. This endangered Colorado species has been reintroduced to major rivers around the state.

ART WOLFE

23 ILLINOIS RIVER MOOSE VIEWING SITE

Description: A tall ridge overlooks an extensive willow bottom along the Illinois River, providing an excellent vantage point for viewing moose in the willows below. A fifty-foot-high observation tower is proposed.

Viewing Information: Excellent opportunity to view moose among the willow thickets, and deer and elk in timber and meadows. Watch for nesting songbirds in the willow thickets, especially yellow and Wilson's warblers. Ducks include mallards and green-winged teal. Active beaver ponds. May be the best moose viewing site in North Park. Best viewing June 1 to October 30.

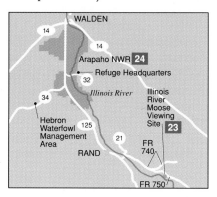

Ownership: USFS (303-723-8204)
Size: 600 acres
Closest Town: Rand
Directions: See map this page

24 ARAPAHO NATIONAL WILDLIFE REFUGE

Description: Open ponds and irrigated meadows offer excellent habitat for nesting waterfowl, shorebirds, and marsh birds. Upland areas of sagebrush flats and knolls.

Viewing Information: Spring and summer offer outstanding viewing of waterfowl, shore, and marsh birds. Peak waterfowl migration in late May. Sage grouse, pronghorn, prairie dogs, and mule deer utilize upland sagebrush areas. Summer raptors include Swainson's hawks, northern harriers, and kestrels. Golden eagles are resident. Muskrats, Wyoming ground squirrels, jackrabbits, and coyotes are all common. Moose and elk are found along Illinois River riparian area of refuge. A six-mile self-guided auto tour (with accompanying brochure available from refuge headquarters) provides an excellent introduction to both upland and wetland habitats and species. Additional waterfowl and shorebird viewing at the BLM's 2,500-acre Hebron Waterfowl Area.

Ownership: BLM, USFWS (303-723-8202)
Size: 18,253 acres
Closest Town: Walden
Directions: See map this page

Description: Mountain riparian area of kettle lakes and beaver ponds. Lodgepole pine and spruce/fir forests completely surround the lakes, with willow bottoms around the beaver ponds. Electric motor or hand-propelled boats only.

Viewing Information: Watch for buffleheads, mallards, ring-necked ducks, and green-winged teal. Many broad-tailed hummingbirds inhabit the campground as well as chipmunks, golden-mantled ground squirrels, and goshawks. Songbirds include yellow-rumped warblers, white-crowned sparrows, western wood pewees, Cassin's finches, and ruby-crowned kinglets. Raptors include red-tailed hawks and harriers. Elk, deer, and porcupines may be seen in the evening from the road.

Ownership: USFS (303-723-8204)
Size: 1,000 acres
Closest Town: Walden
Directions: See map this page

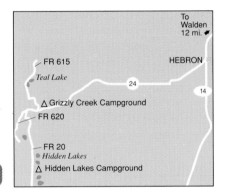

The Illinois River meanders through the Arapaho National Wildlife Refuge in northwest Colorado. Moose can be viewed in the refuge and surrounding area.

JACK OLSON

 26 BIG CREEK LAKES

Description: High mountain lakes surrounded by forests of lodgepole pine and spruce/fir coming down to the water's edge. Good hiking trails lead through a glacial moraine with several kettle lakes. Open mountain meadows with alder/willow riparian zones. Outstanding scenic area with extensive recreational opportunities.

Viewing Information: Excellent opportunity to view ospreys. Loons have been sighted on the lake in the fall. Watch for ducks on the kettle lakes, including buffleheads. Other water-associated birds include black-crowned night-herons, great blue herons, killdeer, kingfishers, and spotted sandpipers. Sharp-shinned, Swainson's, and red-tailed hawks are common raptors. Lots of songbirds in the woods and riparian areas. Mammals include marmots, pikas, and chickarees; lots of beaver activity in the area. Watch for moose among the willows, as well as deer and elk.

Ownership: USFS (303-723-8204)
Size: 600 acres
Closest Town: Walden
Directions: See map this page

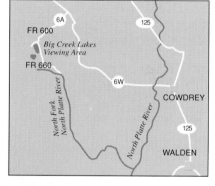

Fish-eating ospreys typically nest in trees. However, the ospreys found in the Big Creek Lakes area nest on a manmade platform constructed in a tree.

MARK A. AUTH/N.E. STOCK

NORTH CENTRAL REGION

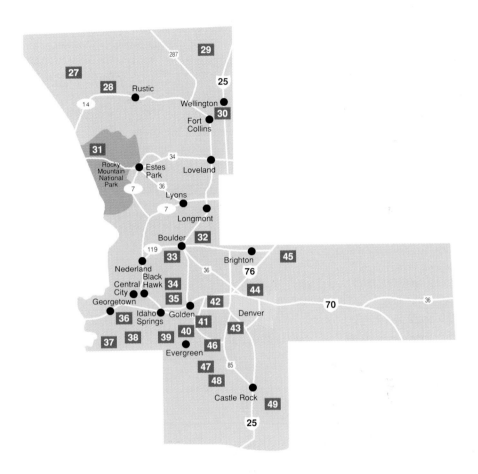

SITE 27	LARAMIE RIVER ROAD	**SITE 38**	MOUNT EVANS HIGHWAY
SITE 28	BIG BEND CAMPGROUND	**SITE 39**	ELK MEADOW PARK
SITE 29	HAMILTON RESERVOIR	**SITE 40**	LAIR O' THE BEAR
SITE 30	FORT COLLINS GREENBELT	**SITE 41**	MORRISON HOGBACK HAWK WATCH
SITE 31	ROCKY MOUNTAIN NATIONAL PARK	**SITE 42**	WHEAT RIDGE GREENBELT
SITE 32	SAWHILL AND WALDEN PONDS	**SITE 43**	SOUTH PLATTE RIVER GREEENWAY
SITE 33	MESA TRAIL	**SITE 44**	ROCKY MOUNTAIN ARSENAL
SITE 34	GOLDEN GATE CANYON STATE PARK	**SITE 45**	BARR LAKE STATE PARK
SITE 35	WHITE RANCH PARK	**SITE 46**	CHATFIELD STATE PARK
SITE 36	GEORGETOWN BIGHORN VIEWING SITE	**SITE 47**	WATERTON CANYON
SITE 37	GUANELLA PASS	**SITE 48**	ROXBOROUGH STATE PARK
		SITE 49	CASTLEWOOD CANYON STATE PARK

 LARAMIE RIVER ROAD

Description: A scenic drive with the mountains of the Rawah Wilderness rising to the west of the river. Primarily dirt road through upper montane coniferous woodlands with some stands of aspen. Meadows and willow riparian areas along the river. The road may be closed by snow.

Viewing Information: Good chance to see moose in willow bottoms, with best viewing where the road is elevated above the river. Golden eagles are visible soaring above ledges. You may see goshawks along the road. Coniferous forest songbirds include gray and Steller's jays, western tanagers, crossbills, and grosbeaks. MacGillivray's, Wilson's, and yellow warblers nest in the willows. Marmots inhabit rock outcroppings to the west. Pronghorn and elk may also be seen.

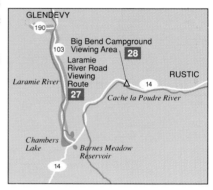

Ownership: PVT, USFS (303-498-1375)
Size: Fifteen-mile drive
Closest Town: Rustic
Directions: See map this page

 BIG BEND CAMPGROUND

Description: Steep, south-facing slope on the north side of the Poudre Canyon. Bitterbrush and sagebrush uplands with scattered Douglas-fir, ponderosa pine, and junipers. Prescribed burns have reduced shrubs and promoted the growth of grass and forbs. For additional information, stop at the visitor information site on CO 14 three miles west of its intersection with U.S. 287.

Viewing Information: Excellent bighorn sheep viewing along rocky slopes on the north side of the highway, across the road from the viewing station. Bighorn sheep are sometimes found right on the road. Stay within the viewing site to avoid disturbing the animals.

Ownership: USFS (303-482-3822)
Size: Ten acres
Closest Town: Rustic
Directions: See map above

29 HAMILTON RESERVOIR

Description: Shortgrass prairie surrounds Hamilton Reservoir, with the Rawhide Power Plant on the north side. Visitors must view only from the parking lot and from the viewing area on the south shore. Please stay off the dam.

Viewing Information: Excellent site to view waterfowl and waterbirds October through March. A variety of ducks sometimes includes oldsquaws, surf and white-winged scoters, Barrow's and common goldeneyes, and common and hooded mergansers. Loons can be seen here; western and Clark's grebes visible May through September. Watch for bald eagles November through February, golden eagles year round, and ospreys and peregrine falcons during spring and fall migration. Best raptor site is west of the viewing area, where they roost on fence posts and power poles. Merlins can be seen December through March on fences and phone lines along the road into the parking area. When water level is low, beach flats attract a variety of shorebirds. There is a small herd of bison on the grounds.

Ownership: PVT (303-484-2836)
Size: 500 acres
Closest Town: Wellington
Directions: See map this page

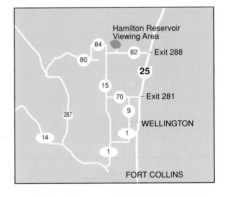

Eared grebes build nests on shallow ponds and marshes. One of five grebe species that migrate through Hamilton Reservoir, the eared grebe nests in colonies at several sites around the state.

SHERM SPOELSTRA

30 FORT COLLINS GREENBELT

Description: Excellent cottonwood/willow riparian corridor through an urban area. Paved trail parallels the Poudre River through Fort Collins, traversing residential, gravel mining, and industrial areas. Numerous public access points. The Environmental Learning Center is open from dawn to dusk seven days a week, featuring interpretive information and displays, nature trail, and a raptor rehabilitation program. It encompasses 200 acres of river bottomland and wetlands.

Viewing Information: Outstanding opportunity to view wildlife in an urban environment. Active red fox dens, four beaver colonies, mule and white-tailed deer, raccoons, fox squirrels, muskrats, and ground squirrels. As many as 206 bird species have been recorded. Excellent for riparian birds in spring and summer. Great waterfowl and waterbird viewing along the river includes Canada geese, a variety of ducks, great blue herons (heronry nearby), cormorants, and numerous shorebirds. Bald and golden eagles visit the area; great horned owls are commonly heard and seen. Site of Operation Osprey release program.

Ownership: City of Fort Collins (303-491-1661)
Size: 8.2 miles one way
Closest Town: Fort Collins
Directions: See map this page

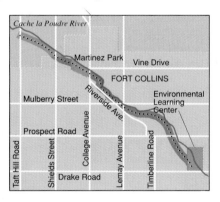

A familiar masked mammal in both urban and rural locales, the raccoon leaves hand-like tracks along wet shorelines.
DENNIS HENRY

31 ROCKY MOUNTAIN NATIONAL PARK

Description: A premier wildlife viewing site, this national park straddling the Continental Divide offers outstanding mountain scenery and incredible vistas. Numerous habitats encompassed by the park—ponderosa pine, Douglas-fir, and aspen forests; mountain meadows; mountain riparian; subalpine spruce/fir forest; and alpine tundra—support a diversity of wildlife. Trail Ridge Road, open summer only, is the highest paved through-highway in the U.S. and provides excellent tundra viewing. The drier eastern slope of the park contrasts with the wet willow bottoms of the Kawuneeche Valley on the western slope. The headwaters of the Colorado River rise from the park's west side.

Viewing Information: Large herds of elk and bighorn sheep are visible in meadows and on mountainsides. You may see mule deer, beavers, coyotes, and river otters. Watch for moose among the willows of the west side. The mountain forests have an abundance of songbirds and small mammals, most noticeably the attention-demanding gray and Steller's jays, Clark's nutcrackers, chipmunks, and golden-mantled ground squirrels. Good chance to see bighorn sheep, marmots, pikas, and ptarmigan along Trail Ridge Road. For detailed and current wildlife viewing information, stop by one of the park's visitor centers. Many interpretive programs offered.

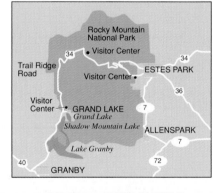

Ownership: NPS (303-586-2371)
Size: 265,649 acres
Closest Town: Estes Park/Grand Lake
Directions: See map this page

Rocky Mountain National Park is an excellent place to view tundra—the land above treeline. Snowmelt from the Never Summer Range, pictured here, feeds the headwaters of the Colorado River.

DAN PEHA

Canada geese flourish in Colorado. Their in-flight V-formations and familiar honking make them especially popular among state wildlife watchers. TOM TIETZ

Description: A network of ponds formed from reclaimed gravel pits and surrounding marshes offers excellent habitat for many bird species. Riparian woodlands on the shore and along Boulder Creek, with brushy open areas.

Viewing Information: A great many ducks and waterbirds arrive on the ponds in winter and during migration. Shorebirds are attracted to sandbars and mud flats when water levels drop. Tundra swans may be seen in fall. Marsh birds include sora and Virginia rails, common snipe, white-faced ibis, and American bitterns. Cottonwood Marsh is a good site for herons, grebes, ducks, geese, and yellow-headed and red-winged blackbirds. An abundance of songbirds in riparian areas. Raptors include great horned owls, red-tailed and rough-legged hawks, northern harriers, kestrels, and northern shrikes.

Ownership: Boulder County, City of Boulder (303-441-3408/441-3950)
Size: 113 acres
Closest Town: Boulder
Directions: See map this page

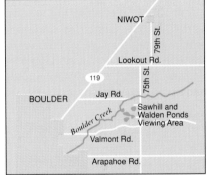

The famed Flatirons form the backdrop for Boulder's Sawhill Ponds. The reclaimed gravel pits boast a diverse population of marsh birds. D. ROBERT FRANZ

33 MESA TRAIL

Description: The south end of this well-marked trail begins along South Boulder Creek in shortgrass prairie intermixed with large patches of tallgrass. Lower elevations have sumac, chokecherry, hawthorn, and juniper. Trail winds through ponderosa pine/Douglas-fir forest with riparian vegetation along numerous canyons. North access in Boulder's Chautauqua Park.

Viewing Information: On its course through a transition zone, the trail offers good opportunities to see a diverse mix of plains and mountain species. Excellent raptor watching features golden eagles, great horned owls, prairie and peregrine falcons, goshawks, and Cooper's and red-tailed hawks. Respect closures for raptor nesting. Canyon bottoms are very good for migratory songbirds May/June and August/September. Watch also for Steller's jays, magpies, ravens, and turkey vultures. Deer are visible throughout, but best viewing is from the south trailhead to the National Center for Atmospheric Research (NCAR). Watch for coyotes, and you may see sign of mountain lions year-round and black bears August through November. Small mammals include Abert's and rock squirrels, golden-mantled ground squirrels, chipmunks, and cottontails.

Ownership: City of Boulder (303-441-3408)
Size: 6.7 miles one way
Closest Town: Boulder
Directions: See map this page

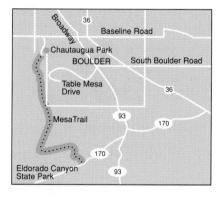

Rock squirrels inhabit rocky country where they can find the vegetation they eat, like this Indian paintbrush. The rock squirrels' loud whistle can help you locate them among the rocks.

DENNIS HENRY

34 | GOLDEN GATE CANYON STATE PARK

Description: This foothills park offers varied habitats, including mountain meadows and wooded slopes of mixed conifer and aspen. Elevations range from 7,600 to 10,400 feet. There are sixty miles of hiking trails within the park, and from Panorama Point visitors have scenic views along nearly 100 miles of the Front Range from Pikes Peak to Longs Peak. Visitor center with interpretive displays. Brochures available.

Viewing Information: Excellent birding site easily accessible from the Denver metro area. Songbirds are abundant in summer. In addition to gray and Steller's jays and Clark's nutcrackers, watch for chickadees, juncos, sapsuckers, western tanagers, grosbeaks, bluebirds, nighthawks, poorwills, lazuli buntings, and tree, barn, and violet-green swallows. Raptors include eagles, prairie falcons, various owls and hawks. Deer and elk are often seen. Beaver viewing deck along Ralston Creek. Trout viewing pond near the visitor center.

Ownership: CDPOR (303-592-1502)
Size: 11,000 acres
Closest Town: Golden
Directions: See map this page

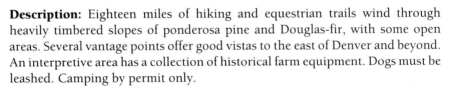

35 | WHITE RANCH PARK

Description: Eighteen miles of hiking and equestrian trails wind through heavily timbered slopes of ponderosa pine and Douglas-fir, with some open areas. Several vantage points offer good vistas to the east of Denver and beyond. An interpretive area has a collection of historical farm equipment. Dogs must be leashed. Camping by permit only.

Viewing Information: You're unlikely to see bears, mountain lions, or bobcats, but you may see their tracks and sign. Keep your eyes open for deer, elk, and wild turkeys as well as squirrels and Steller's jays.

Ownership: Jefferson County Open Space
(303-271-5925)
Size: 3,040 acres
Closest Town: Golden
Directions: See map above

53

36 | GEORGETOWN BIGHORN VIEWING SITE

Description: Developed interpretive site overlooking nearly year-round bighorn sheep habitat. The viewing tower gives excellent views of bighorn sheep habitat across Interstate 70. The tower has coin-operated viewing scopes. The donation helps maintain the site and develop interpretive information. When you get near, tune your radio to AM 530 for wildlife viewing information.

Viewing Information: Between 175 and 200 bighorn sheep utilize the habitat, often standing very close to the interstate. Bighorn sheep can be seen here nearly every month of the year, but the best viewing is fall, winter, and spring.

Ownership: City of Georgetown, BLM, CDOW (303-569-2555)
Size: N/A
Closest Town: Georgetown
Directions: See map this page

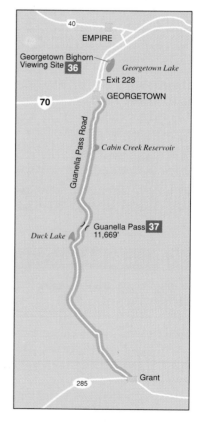

37 | GUANELLA PASS

Description: The pass offers year-round access to alpine habitat plus spectacular views of Mt. Evans and Mt. Bierstadt. The route is a scenic byway.

Viewing Information: Accessible opportunity to view alpine habitat and wildlife year-round. Possibly the best spot in the U.S. for viewing white-tailed ptarmigan. Bighorn sheep, mountain goats, and elk are visible on mountain slopes and in the basin below the summit. Jays, nutcrackers, grosbeaks, and blue grouse reside in high-elevation forests year-round. Watch also for Abert's squirrels and chickarees. In September raptors and swallows migrating south fly low over the top of the pass.

Ownership: PVT, USFS (303-567-2901)
Size: Twenty-six miles of road
Closest Town: Georgetown/Grant

Directions: See map this page

Description: The Mt. Evans Highway is the highest paved road in the United States. The fourteen-mile drive from Echo Lake to the summit parking area offers spectacular scenic views as well as dependable wildlife viewing opportunities. Plan on three to four hours to complete the round trip. Good tundra viewing in close proximity to a major metropolitan area. The road ends just before the 14,264-foot summit of Mt. Evans. The paved highway is extremely narrow and winding; use caution when stopping to view animals. Road is closed by snow, early fall through late spring. Stay on trails around Summit Lake to protect delicate vegetation.

Viewing Information: Beginning at Echo Lake at 10,700 feet, the first few miles of the highway traverse subalpine forest, home to chickarees, blue grouse, gray jays, and Clark's nutcrackers. Many songbirds move to this zone in late summer because of abundant food resources. The 1.1-mile trail at the Mount Goliath Natural Area passes through a stand of gnarled bristlecone pine, among the oldest living organisms on earth. Good views from here of elk in meadows and on open slopes. Mountain goats and bighorn sheep often visible on or near the road. Watch rocky slopes above timberline for mountain goats. At Summit Lake a short trail leads along the lake with a good chance to see or hear pikas, ptarmigan, marmots, American pipits, and brown-capped rosy finches. Wildflowers are abundant.

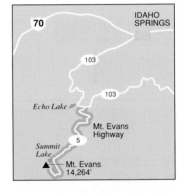

Ownership: City of Denver, USFS (303-567-2901)
Size: Fourteen miles one way
Closest Town: Idaho Springs
Directions: See map this page

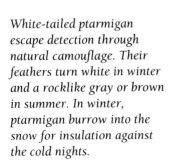

White-tailed ptarmigan escape detection through natural camouflage. Their feathers turn white in winter and a rocklike gray or brown in summer. In winter, ptarmigan burrow into the snow for insulation against the cold nights.
WENDY SHATTIL/BOB ROZINSKI

39 ELK MEADOW PARK

Description: The variety of mountain habitats in this park—meadows, ponderosa pine and Douglas-fir woodlands, aspen groves, montane zone and the exposed, subalpine terrain around the summit of 9,708-foot Bergen Peak—supports a variety of wildlife. Numerous marked hiking trails. Good scenic views from various points in the park. Dogs must be leashed.

Viewing Information: In the lower elevation meadows watch for elk, deer, coyotes, Wyoming ground squirrels, and other small mammals. The ponderosa pine forest is home to Abert's squirrels and chipmunks. Ravens are common. Look for red-tailed and Swainson's hawks soaring on thermals over open areas. The park encompasses several wildlife preserves, including the Bergen Peak State Wildlife Area. Stay on the trail in the spring during elk calving to avoid stressing the animals. In early summer the meadow wildflowers are outstanding.

Ownership: CDOW, Denver Mountain Parks, Jefferson County Open Space (303-271-5925)
Size: 1,140 acres
Closest Town: Evergreen/Bergen Park
Directions: See map this page

The Abert's squirrel is one of the few Colorado animals associated exclusively with a single plant community. Ponderosa pines provide these "tassel-eared" squirrels with all the essentials—food, shelter, and nest sites. WENDY SHATTIL/BOB ROZINSKI

40 LAIR O' THE BEAR

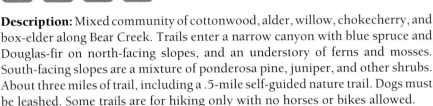

Description: Mixed community of cottonwood, alder, willow, chokecherry, and box-elder along Bear Creek. Trails enter a narrow canyon with blue spruce and Douglas-fir on north-facing slopes, and an understory of ferns and mosses. South-facing slopes are a mixture of ponderosa pine, juniper, and other shrubs. About three miles of trail, including a .5-mile self-guided nature trail. Dogs must be leashed. Some trails are for hiking only with no horses or bikes allowed.

Viewing Information: Active beaver colony along the creek. Elk viewing best in fall and winter. Dippers are visible along the creek. Good site for songbirds, including warblers, orioles, magpies, western tanagers, and Steller's jays. Watch for kestrels and woodland hawks.

Ownership: Jefferson County Open Space (303-271-5925)
Size: 319 acres
Closest Town: Kittredge
Directions: See map this page

41 MORRISON HOGBACK HAWK WATCH

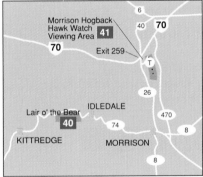

Description: An open site above the town of Morrison atop the Dakota Hogback stretching north and south along the Front Range west of Denver. Beginning at the parking lot at the southeast corner of Interstate 70 and CO 26, take the trail to the top of the hogback. The observation site is about a thirty-minute walk from the parking lot. Good views of migrating raptors and the Denver metro area to the east.

Viewing Information: Migration corridor for a variety of raptors. More than 2,000 birds, representing eighteen species, can be seen in an eight-week period in spring. Watch for eagles and hawks. Later in April look for hawks, kestrels, merlins, and falcons. Turkey vultures and ospreys are often visible.

Ownership: Jefferson County Open Space
(303-697-1873)
Size: Thirty-minute walk
Closest Town: Morrison
Directions: See map above

42 WHEAT RIDGE GREENBELT

Description: A paved trail meanders through an urban greenbelt following Clear Creek. Cottonwood/willow community along the creek borders open meadows, offering excellent edge habitat. A boardwalk through a marshy area of Prospect Park allows good access to this habitat. Four reservoirs west of the park provide open water year-round for waterfowl viewing. Greenbelt access is from Johnson Park, Wheat Ridge Park, Prospect Park, and Youngfield Street between 38th and 44th avenues.

Viewing Information: An important wildlife corridor and outstanding opportunity for urban wildlife viewing. More than 180 bird species have been recorded here. An abundance of songbirds are attracted to the riparian zones along the creek—woodpeckers, warblers, grosbeaks, tanagers, flycatchers, vireos. Year-round waterfowl viewing on open creek and reservoirs. Many wetland birds, common snipe, sora, and Virginia rails. Watch for dippers along the creek in winter. Mammals include muskrats, red foxes, and raccoons. Beavers reside in the Wheat Ridge Park and Johnson Park areas.

Ownership: City of Wheat Ridge (303-423-2626)
Size: 270 acres
Closest Town: Wheat Ridge
Directions: See map this page

The male western tanager is one of Colorado's most colorful species. Western tanagers migrate through urban habitats along the Front Range en route to their nesting area in coniferous forests.
WENDY SHATTIL/BOB ROZINSKI

Description: Thirty-mile paved bike and walking path following the South Platte River from Chatfield State Park to the river's confluence with Clear Creek winds through Denver metropolitan area. A variety of urban landscapes includes light industrial, residential, open space, suburban parks. Cottonwood riparian zones along much of the river. Excellent urban wildlife corridor. Sixteen municipal parks are located along the greenway, including South Platte Park in Littleton with the only remaining piece of the South Platte River through Denver that isn't channelized. Much of the river is also boatable by nonmotorized craft. There are numerous trail access points along the route.

Viewing Information: Ducks—including mallards, gadwalls, shovelers, hooded mergansers, and goldeneyes—are visible on the river, especially in winter. Watch for great blue herons, black-crowned night-herons, and belted kingfishers at water's edge. Many mammals use this riverine corridor, including beavers, musk-rats, red foxes, raccoons, skunks, deer. Numerous songbirds inhabit the cotton-wood/willow woodlands along the river, especially in spring and summer.

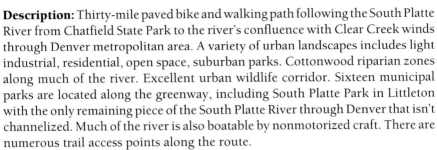

Ownership: Multiple counties and municipalities (303-698-1322)
Size: Thirty miles one way
Closest Town: Metro Denver
Directions: See map this page

The South Platte River provides semi-arid, urban Denver with a riparian corridor that is rich in wildlife.
BUD SMITH

44 | ROCKY MOUNTAIN ARSENAL

Description: A small portion of the 17,000 acres of the Rocky Mountain Arsenal was set aside for chemical and weapons production, carried on here for forty years. Production areas were surrounded by a one-mile buffer that created an "island of habitat" for wildlife as the Denver metro area grew. Today an amazing diversity of birds, mammals, reptiles, and amphibians inhabits this pocket of undeveloped land on the edge of a major metropolitan area. Ponds and lakes, grasslands and riparian zones. Arsenal access is currently restricted to guided tours except for the bald eagle viewing blind.

Viewing Information: White-tailed and mule deer are highly visible, as are coyotes, prairie dogs, Canada geese, and many species of songbirds and waterfowl. Prairie dog colonies attract a variety of predators, including coyotes, badgers, ferruginous hawks, and a large population of wintering bald eagles. In summer burrowing owls nest in the prairie dog towns. Passerines include northern orioles, flickers, wrens, and warblers. Lakes, ponds, and surrounding marshy areas attract ducks, geese, coots, grebes, herons, avocets, and other birds. A viewing blind overlooks a bald eagle winter roost.

Ownership: US Army/USFWS
(303-289-0132)
Size: 17,000 acres
Closest Town: Denver, Commerce City
Directions: See map this page

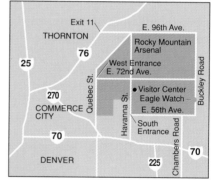

In winter, bald eagles and other birds of prey visit the Rocky Mountain Arsenal. The Arsenal offers snowy Front Range vistas and unparalleled wildlife viewing opportunities within ten miles of downtown Denver.
WENDY SHATTIL/BOB ROZINSKi

45 BARR LAKE STATE PARK

Description: A premier birdwatching site. Bird records from Barr Lake date back more than 100 years with over 300 species recorded. Combining three habitats—open water, shoreline cottonwood/willow woodlands, and grassland—the park is home to a diversity of wildlife. Interpretive programs and displays are offered at the Wildlife Center and through park headquarters. Wooden boardwalks and viewing gazebo are found along the lakeshore.

Viewing Information: The lake attracts an array of waterfowl and waterbirds, including geese, white pelicans, grebes, coots, and numerous species of ducks. The shoreline riparian area offers nesting for owls, hawks, songbirds, and wading birds. Great blue herons, black-crowned night-herons, and double-crested cormorants populate a rookery here, but the most famous residents are the pair of nesting bald eagles. Mule deer roam the park. Red foxes den each spring in grassland areas surrounding the lake. Watch for a variety of small mammals—fox squirrels, thirteen-lined ground squirrels, muskrats, pocket gophers, and raccoons. In spring and summer listen for chorus frogs in the ponds along the nature trail. Bullsnakes and several species of turtle also live here.

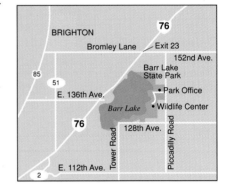

Ownership: CDPOR (303-659-6005)
Size: 2,609 acres
Closest Town: Brighton
Directions: See map this page

This viewing gazebo at Barr Lake State Park, is one of Colorado's most popular bird-watching sites. Barr Lake is one of the few state locations where nesting bald eagles may be viewed.

BUD SMITH

61

46 CHATFIELD STATE PARK

Description: Located where the prairie meets the foothills, this state park attracts both grassland and mountain wildlife, plus migratory birds moving along the edge of the Front Range. Grassland areas surround a 1,100-acre reservoir. Plum and Deer creeks, the South Platte River, and the Highline Canal traverse the park, supporting an extensive cottonwood/willow/box-elder riparian community. Large cattail marsh along Plum Creek. A wetlands being developed near the west boundary has an observation platform and interpretive trails. Viewing blinds and scopes at the heronry allow eye level viewing of nesting herons and cormorants.

Viewing Information: More than 300 species of birds have been recorded here. A premier spot in Colorado for woodland birds and migrants: house wrens, wood-pewees, swallows, vireos, woodpeckers, eight species of swallows, and thirty-two species of warblers. Good waterfowl viewing on the reservoir in spring and fall. Watch also for red-winged and yellow-headed blackbirds, coots, grebes, loons (in fall), and kingfishers. Great blue herons and double-crested cormorants are highly visible. Occasional migrant osprey. Lots of beavers and mule deer.

Ownership: CDPOR (303-791-7275)
Size: 5,600 acres
Closest Town: Littleton
Directions: See map below

47 WATERTON CANYON

Description: Lower canyon access follows a road along the South Platte River to the beginning of the Colorado Trail. The road was built on the old bed of the Denver, South Park, and Pacific Narrow Gauge Railroad. Very popular for mountain biking. Habitat changes with elevation, from montane shrublands to Douglas fir/ponderosa pine. Cottonwoods, willow thickets, and box-elder along the river. The canyon is accessible by foot, horseback, or bike only. Dogs and motorized vehicles are prohibited.

Viewing Information: The cliffs offer good nesting for golden eagles and turkey vultures. Watch for Cooper's and sharp-shinned hawks in higher-elevation coniferous forests. Songbirds in riparian areas. Bighorn sheep sometimes visible near or on the road. Watch also for mule deer. Good chance to see dippers along the river. Wintering bald eagles patrol the river from a major roosting site at Cheesman Reservoir.

Ownership: USFS, Denver Water Dept., PVT(303-236-5371)
Size: Six miles
Closest Town: Littleton
Directions: See map opposite page

48 ROXBOROUGH STATE PARK

Description: Characterized by red rock formations, Roxborough is located in a transition zone between plains and foothills. Grasslands and oak brush shrublands mixed with wet meadows; cottonwood/box-elder communities along Little Willow Creek. Ridgetops and slopes of Carpenter Peak feature ponderosa pine/Douglas-fir. Several aspen groves in moist, sheltered areas, well below the species' usual altitude. Excellent geological site.

Viewing Information: Watch for mule deer, elk, coyotes, and many small mammals. You may see signs of bobcat, mountain lion, and bear. Good raptor viewing. Prairie falcons currently nesting in former peregrine falcon nest site. Watch also for golden eagles, kestrels, and red-tailed hawks. The park checklist includes over 140 bird species. Reptiles include bullsnakes, rattlesnakes, hog-nose and garter snakes, box turtles, chorus frogs, fence lizards, and yellow-bellied racers.

Ownership: CDPOR (303-973-3959)
Size: 1,620 acres
Closest Town: Littleton
Directions: See map opposite page

49  **CASTLEWOOD CANYON STATE PARK**

Description: A steep-walled "prairie canyon" cut by Cherry Creek offers dramatic terrain and habitat for cliff-dwelling raptors and other birds. Rocky canyon top with ponderosa pine and scrub oak, dramatic palisades, and panoramic views up and down the canyon. Ten miles of hiking trails; maps are available. A visitor center is scheduled to open by fall of 1992. Do not climb on the unstable ruins of the Castlewood Dam, which was washed out in a 1936 flood.

Viewing Information: Excellent place to spot turkey vultures lazing on the thermals. Sometimes as many as 100 will congregate above the canyon. Watch also for golden eagles (nesting nearby), as well as red-tailed, Swainson's, and ferruginous hawks. Site of a unique "dry heronry" with great blue herons nesting in pine trees. Avoid approaching the nests as the herons are easily disturbed. Saw-whet owls and nesting great horned owls. Watch for dippers along the creek. Western rattlesnakes sun among the rocks. Fence lizards also common. Look for deer atop the canyon or along the creek. A variety of small mammals—cottontails, squirrels, deer mice, beavers, and muskrats—is found along the creek.

Ownership: CDPOR (303-688-7505)
Size: 870 acres
Closest Town: Franktown
Directions: See map this page

Turkey vultures, nature's recyclers, eat animal carcasses. Their feather-less heads allow easy access to their meals and prevent bacterial buildup. Dozens of these large vultures regularly soar above Castlewood Canyon.

D. ROBERT FRANZ

NORTHEAST REGION

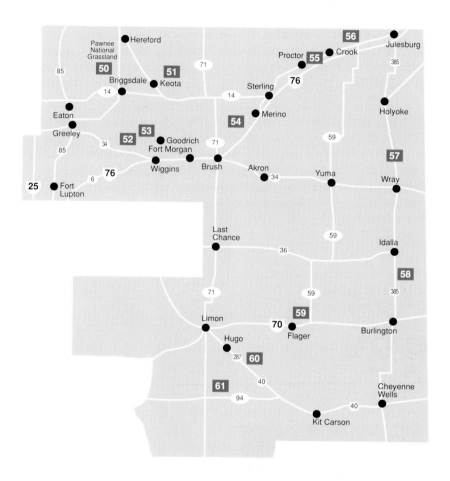

50 | PAWNEE NATIONAL GRASSLAND BIRDING LOOP

Description: A premier prairie birdwatching tour; the bird checklist includes over 200 species, including grassland birds, migrant waterfowl, and shorebirds. The boxelder/willow riparian area at the Crow Valley Campground is like an oasis amid the dry shortgrass prairie, attracting a variety of eastern and mountain birds. The brochure, "Birding on the Pawnee by Automobile or Mountain Bike," is available from the Pawnee National Grassland Headquarters, 2009 9th St., Greeley, C0, 80631.

Viewing Information: Good chance to see and hear "larking" (singing courtship flight) of lark buntings, horned larks, meadowlarks, and longspurs late May through June. Prairie birds to watch for include mountain plovers, chestnut-collared and McCown's longspurs, burrowing owls, and long-billed curlews. In the campground, streamside riparian habitat attracts a great variety of birds April through June and late August through October, including warblers, thrushes, flycatchers, orioles, and kingbirds. Murphy Reservoir offers good shorebird and waterfowl viewing.

Ownership: USFS, PVT
(303-353-5004)
Size: Thirty-six-mile self-guided tour
Closest Town: Briggsdale
Directions: See map this page

GR 104

57   77

GR 69

GR 96

96

GR 61

Crow Valley
Campground △

14

BRIGGSDALE

Pawnee National Grassland

The long-billed curlew's in-flight cry sounds just like its name. The curlew's long, curved beak enables it to probe through sand and mud for crustaceans, mollusks, insects, and worms.

W. PERRY CONWAY

51  **PAWNEE BUTTES**

Description: The Pawnee National Grassland is a remnant of the plains grassland that once covered eastern Colorado. Federal lands are intermingled with private ownership, and some blocks are grazed and cultivated. Dramatic high points are the Pawnee Buttes, a pair of sandstone formations towering 250 feet above the surrounding prairie. The grassland is divided into two parcels. The buttes are in the eastern parcel.

Viewing Information: Such raptors as kestrels, prairie falcons, golden eagles, and Swainson's and ferruginous hawks nest on surrounding escarpments in isolated trees, and on the steep sides of the buttes. Do not climb on the buttes or escarpments during sensitive nesting periods from early spring through midsummer. Watch for pronghorn, mule deer, coyotes, prairie dogs, jackrabbits, and kangaroo rats (at night). Grassland reptiles include short-horned lizards, bullsnakes, fence lizards, and western rattlesnakes. Excellent mammal fossils dating from the Miocene and Oligocene periods have been found at the buttes. Fossils and cultural artifacts are protected by federal law.

Ownership: PVT, USFS (303-353-5004)
Size: 775,000 acres
Closest Town: Briggsdale
Directions: See map this page

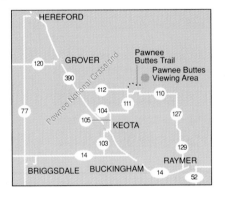

The Pawnee Buttes stand sentinel over northeast Colorado's Pawnee National Grassland. Premier bird watching country, the grassland preserves remnants of the once vast shortgrass prairie. SHERM SPOELSTRA

52 WHITE PELICAN NESTING COLONY

Description: This island in Riverside Reservoir is one of three nesting colonies for white pelicans in the state. Most of the reservoir is closed to the public, but a restricted trail allows limited lakeshore access to view the white pelican nesting site. The island is off-limits. Park along the road. Binoculars are very helpful.

Viewing Information: Excellent opportunity to view white pelicans and their behavior—in air, on water, and nesting. Watch for gulls, cormorants, ducks, and shorebirds among the abundant waterbirds on the reservoir. In winter, bald eagles are visible roosting in cottonwoods around the lake or flying over the water.

Ownership: PVT, BLM (719-275-0631)
Size: 3,150 acres
Closest Town: Wiggins
Directions: See map this page

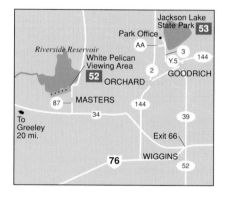

53 JACKSON LAKE STATE PARK

Description: Plains reservoir surrounded by grasslands and fields with scattered cottonwoods and sandy beaches along the shore.

Viewing Information: The reservoir is a major stopover for migrant shorebirds, bald eagles, waterfowl, and other water birds, especially white pelicans. Watch fields along the east side of the reservoir for sandhill cranes in spring and fall. Large groups of as many as 400 white pelicans can be seen during migration. Watch for shore and wading birds, gulls, and waterfowl especially in dry years when lowered water levels expose sandy beaches and mud flats. Occasional duck flocks numbering 20,000 birds. Major bald eagle site with excellent viewing opportunities in the spring. Sometimes as many as forty will gather on spring days when the birds are preparing to migrate. Grassland areas attract plovers, longspurs, and horned larks.

Ownership: CDPOR (303-645-2551)
Size: 2,540 acres
Closest Town: Wiggins
Directions: See map above

Five hundred pairs of white pelicans nest at Riverside Reservoir. Sound management practices resulted in population growth of the big-billed birds, and white pelicans have been removed from the state's endangered species list. HARRY ENGELS

54 | PREWITT RESERVOIR STATE WILDLIFE AREA

Description: Grassland and old cultivated fields surround the reservoir, with patches of cottonwoods along the shore. Lowered water levels in dry years expose a sandy beach that can provide good habitat for shorebirds.

Viewing Information: A good spot to see white pelicans, sometimes hundreds at once. Many great blue herons, coots, and ducks. Check the shoreline cottonwoods for flickers, red-headed woodpeckers, kingbirds, and other passerines. Watch for sandhill cranes stopping to feed and rest here during migrations. Bald eagles use the area in winter.

Ownership: CDOW (303-842-3124)
Size: 2,900 acres
Closest Town: Merino
Directions: See map this page

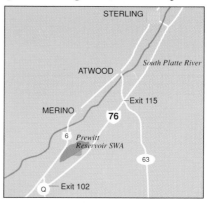

STERLING

ATWOOD

South Platte River

Exit 115

MERINO

76

6 Prewitt
Reservoir SWA

63

Q Exit 102

The coot, a common sight around ponds and marshes, pumps its head back and forth while swimming. The white-billed bird dives below the surface of the water to feed or escape intruders.

TOM TIETZ

55 TAMARACK RANCH STATE WILDLIFE AREA

Description: This site encompasses nearly twenty miles of the South Platte River and a variety of habitats—wooded bottomlands, farmed plots, and sagebrush sandhills. A portion of the grain cut on the plots is left for wildlife.

Viewing Information: In early morning watch for greater prairie-chickens, a Colorado endangered species reintroduced by the CDOW in the uplands on the south side of the river. Plains sharp-tailed grouse, another species endangered in Colorado, are returning naturally. Good site for bobwhite quail and wild turkeys. Watch also for buntings, yellow- and black-billed cuckoos, Bell's vireos, grassland songbirds, and several grosbeaks. Watch for both western and eastern races of some species such as northern orioles and common flickers. U.S. 138 east of Crook may be the best spot in the state to see upland sandpipers. White-tailed deer along river bottoms. Duck Creek State Wildlife Area is nearby.

Ownership: CDOW (303-474-2711)
Size: 14,599 acres
Closest Town: Crook
Directions: See map this page

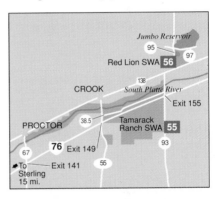

56 RED LION/JUMBO RESERVOIR STATE WILDLIFE AREA

Description: Jumbo Reservoir and the Red Lion State Wildlife Area are surrounded by shortgrass prairie, mud flats, lowland marsh areas, and cottonwood riparian zones. Food plots and shelter belts have been established for upland birds and small mammals. Red Lion is closed during waterfowl nesting.

Viewing Information: Excellent viewing of waterfowl in winter; three teal species seen in spring; Canada, snow, and occasional Ross' and white-fronted geese. Bald eagles and several gull species can be seen in winter. Sandhill cranes visible during spring and fall migrations. Watch for painted turtles. Upland sandpipers fairly common.

Ownership: CDOW (303-474-2711)
Size: 1,498 acres
Closest Town: Crook
Directions: See map above

71

57 | GREATER PRAIRIE-CHICKEN LEKS

Description: Leks, or dancing grounds, are flat, open grassland areas used by successive generations of prairie-chickens during spring courtship. Prairie grassland is essential to provide cover and forage for the birds. All the prairie-chicken leks are on private land. It's possible to drive some county roads north of Wray and see birds from the road. Access to view the leks must be arranged through the CDOW, (303) 484-2836. Groups must arrive at the leks well before dawn and remain in vehicles. Primary viewing mid-March to May at dawn and dusk.

Viewing Information: The spring courtship dance of the greater prairie-chicken is a fascinating sight as the males fluff up, strut, spar, erect the feathers on their heads, and emit a popping or "booming" sound from the air sacs on their necks. Greater prairie-chickens are endangered in Colorado, with the only significant population found here in Yuma County.

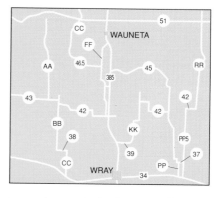

Ownership: PVT (303-484-2836)
Size: N/A
Closest Town: Wray
Directions: See map this page

Found in grassland country with sandy soils, the male greater prairie-chicken boasts a distinctive orange air sac. Its cousin, the lesser prairie-chicken, is characterized by a pink air sac. W. PERRY CONWAY

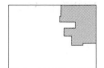

Description: A large complex of habitats including plains grassland, reservoir, agricultural land, and excellent cottonwood/willow lowland riparian areas around the reservoir and along the river. Some remnants of native prairie exist.

Viewing Information: Extensive bird checklist of 287 species is available from CDOW and CDPOR. Songbirds in woodlands near Wagonwheel Campground. Look for strutting wild turkeys in spring at Foster Grove Campground. White pelicans and wading birds at water's edge. Good opportunity to see wood ducks with young in spring and summer. Watch for turkey vultures, beaver, and muskrat on the west end. Wintering bald eagles on the lake and good winter waterfowl viewing. Migrant snow geese visible mid-October to mid-November and in March; sandhill cranes in October at the southwest corner of the lake. Also loons, egrets, herons, white-faced ibis, black terns, tundra swans, white-fronted and snow geese, woodpeckers, eastern bluebirds, orchard orioles, and eastern screech owls. White-tailed deer year round in corn and hay fields.

Ownership: CDOW, PVT, CDPOR (303-354-7306)
Size: 24,000 acres
Closest Town: Idalia
Directions: See map this page

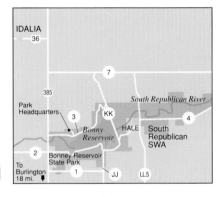

A watery oasis on eastern Colorado's dry plains, Bonny Reservoir is part of an extensive system of riparian and prairie habitats set in a vast agricultural region.
D. ROBERT FRANZ

Found primarily on the state's eastern plains, the white-tailed deer is highly adaptable, but prefers the cover offered by wooded areas. When alarmed, the animal raises its tail like a flag as it flees. CLAUDE STEELMAN

59 FLAGLER RESERVOIR STATE WILDLIFE AREA

Description: Small prairie reservoir surrounded by agricultural land. Reservoir water level fluctuates with irrigation demand. At the upper end is a cattail wetland, with some willow and cottonwood.

Viewing Information: Watch for pheasants and wild turkeys in upland areas. Usually good opportunity to see waterfowl on the reservoir: mallards, pintails, coots, canvasbacks, wigeons, Canada and occasional snow geese. Concentrations of up to 130 white pelicans can be seen in spring and fall. In low water years, there may be some shorebirds. Great blue herons are frequently seen. Golden eagles, Swainson's and red-tailed hawks in migration. Songbirds in riparian areas. Good viewing of grassland songbirds—meadowlarks, lark buntings—and riparian songbirds among cottonwoods and willows in spring and summer. Watch for nighthawks. Spring brings concentrations of turkey vultures. White-tailed and mule deer fairly common.

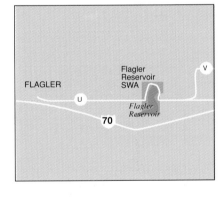

Ownership: CDOW (719-473-2945)
Size: 400 acres
Closest Town: Flagler
Directions: See map this page

Pintails are distinguished by long, pointed tails and prominent white stripes extending up both sides of their heads. The birds are common spring and fall migrants through Colorado.

D. ROBERT FRANZ

60 LADYBIRD REST AREA

Description: An agricultural pasture, formerly shortgrass prairie, across the highway from the rest area. This is private land, so do not enter. Park at the rest area or along the side of the road and watch the pronghorn from your car. Rest area facilities are closed in winter.

Viewing Information: A small herd of pronghorn is visible in the pasture year round.

Ownership: PVT (719-473-2945)
Size: Fifty acres
Closest Town: Hugo
Directions: See map this page

61 HUGO STATE WILDLIFE AREA

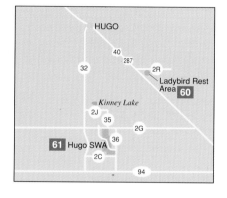

Description: Rolling terrain, primarily shortgrass prairie. Several small spring-fed ponds with scattered stands of cottonwoods. Two low-lying cottonwood/willow riparian areas.

Viewing Information: Good viewing of grassland species. Watch for jackrabbits, and cottontails, coyotes, numerous muskrats on the ponds, pronghorn, and mule and white-tailed deer. Some resident mallards, occasional other ducks in migration. Grassland songbirds include meadowlarks, horned larks, and lark buntings. Numerous mourning doves in wooded areas and red-winged blackbirds in marshy spots. Raptors include Swainson's and rough-legged hawks, and northern harriers.

Ownership: CDOW (719-473-2945)
Size: 2,240 acres
Closest Town: Hugo
Directions: See map above

SOUTHEAST REGION

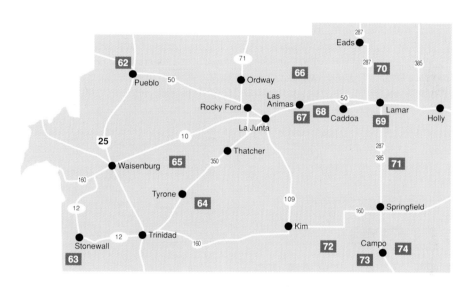

62 PUEBLO GREENWAY

Description: A three-mile paved biking and walking path begins at the Pueblo Nature Center and passes through cottonwood riparian areas along the Arkansas River. The trail ends at Pueblo Reservoir. The nature center has interpretive displays, live animal exhibits, and a naturalist on duty. The Raptor Center can be visited by appointment.

Viewing Information: The nature center's fishing pier overlooks the river, offering the chance to see trout, bass, and other fish. Watch for great blue herons, kingfishers, and a variety of songbirds along the river. Ospreys are visible in spring and fall, bald eagles in winter. There is one active osprey nest at the west end of the reservoir. Numerous ducks, including mergansers and nesting wood ducks, as well as white pelicans, Canada and snow geese, cormorants, and grebes can be seen. Red-tailed and Swainson's hawks are visible in open areas. Mammals include beavers, muskrats, fox squirrels, red foxes, skunks, raccoons, and white-tailed and mule deer.

Ownership: City of Pueblo
(719-545-9114)
Size: Three miles one way
Closest Town: Pueblo
Directions: See map this page

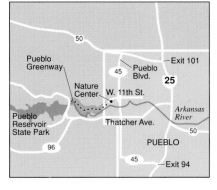

Muskrats often share their ponds with beavers, and many wildlife viewers mistake one for the other. Muskrats—which inhabit the edges of ponds, lakes, and slow-moving streams—are capable swimmers, and they use their long, thin tails like rudders.

MICHAEL S. SAMPLE

Description: Meadows and grasslands surrounded by ponderosa pine forest. Land is private so viewing is from the county road.

Viewing Information: Watch for elk in meadows and open areas along the county road between Stonewall and the New Mexico border. Wild turkeys and bald eagles can be seen along the South Fork of the Purgatoire River. Evening and early morning are best viewing times for elk and wild turkeys. Watch for birds in the meadows and among the pines.

Ownership: PVT (719-561-4909)
Size: Sixteen miles one way
Closest Town: Stonewall
Directions: See map this page

Often spotted in flocks or large family groups, wild turkeys roost above the ground, usually in large trees. Toms display their brilliantly colored wattles and fanned tailfeathers to attract females during the spring breeding season.

TOM TIETZ

79

64 PINON CANYON

Description: The canyon is an area of mixed habitats: shortgrass prairie with scattered pinyon/juniper woodlands, limestone breaks, red sandstone cliffs, cottonwood riparian zones, some aspen, a basalt ridge along the south, and a series of side canyons along the Purgatoire River. You must first stop at the headquarters office forty-one miles northeast of Trinidad on U.S. 350 to get a pass and area map. There is a $10 annual fee.

Viewing Information: Great place to see pronghorn—a herd of about 1,000 live on the Pinon Canyon Military Reservation—as well as 400 to 500 mule deer. Excellent raptor viewing—golden eagles, Swainson's, ferruginous, and red-tailed hawks, and prairie falcons all nest here. Watch also for northern harriers and turkey vultures. Songbirds are common in the grassland riparian areas. Wild turkeys and scaled quail may be seen. Carnivores include coyotes, foxes, and badgers. Beavers along the river; prairie dogs and rabbits in upland areas.

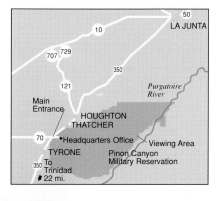

Ownership: US Army (719-579-2752)
Size: 250,000 acres
Closest Town: Trinidad
Directions: See map this page

The grumpy badger's powerful front legs enable this expert excavator to dig out its next meal. Badgers live in open terrain through-out Colorado, especially near colonies of ground-dwelling rodents.

WENDY SHATTIL/BOB ROZINSKI

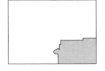

65 APISHAPA STATE WILDLIFE AREA

Description: Uplands of shortgrass prairie with juniper woodlands. Two main rocky, steep-walled canyons cut through the area. The canyons are dotted with junipers; a few cottonwoods are scattered along the river tributaries. Both rims of the Apishapa River Canyon are accessible by vehicle, but roads may not be passable in wet weather. Four-wheel-drive vehicles recommended in bad weather.

Viewing Information: Bighorn sheep inhabit the canyons. Watch for pronghorn, mule deer, and coyotes in grassland areas. Meadowlarks and other grassland songbirds common. Scaled quail and mourning doves are numerous, with some wild turkeys. Reptiles include bullsnakes, rattlesnakes, and short-horned and fence lizards. Watch for red-tailed and Swainson's hawks and golden eagles soaring on the thermals.

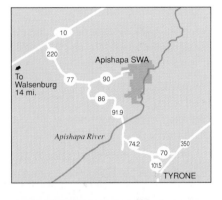

Ownership: CDOW (719-561-4909)
Size: 7,935 acres
Closest Town: Walsenburg
Directions: See map this page

Extremely adaptable, coyotes thrive in a wide range of environments, both urban and wild. These social animals communicate with howls, yips, and barks.

D. ROBERT FRANZ

81

66 ADOBE CREEK RESERVOIR STATE WILDLIFE AREA

Description: Shortgrass prairie surrounds the lake, with stands of tamarisk and cottonwood on the north shore. Portions of the area are closed in winter to protect waterfowl.

Viewing Information: This is a prime prairie birdwatching site with outstanding waterfowl and shorebird viewing. Three to four hundred white pelicans gather here in summer. Endangered least terns nest on an island which is closed to public access. Please respect this rare bird's nesting sensitivity. Thousands of waterfowl use this lake during migration, primarily Canada geese, mallards, pintails, gadwalls, widgeons, and some teal. Snow geese are also seen. Up to 5,000 sandhill cranes stop here during fall migration. Good winter concentrations of bald eagles which roost in the cottonwoods. Occasional golden eagles, and peregrine falcons have been seen here. Excellent chance to see pronghorn on the drive into the area. Watch for mule deer around the lake.

Ownership: CDOW (719-336-4852)
Size: 5,147 acres
Closest Town: Las Animas
Directions: See map this page

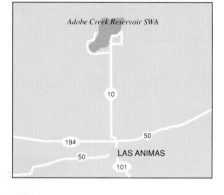

Snow geese make their fall migrations in large numbers. Their largest concentrations occur at southeast Colorado lakes and reservoirs. Snow geese are easily recognized by their white bodies and black wing tips.

D. ROBERT FRANZ

Found in prairie dog colonies where they nest in abandoned burrows, burrowing owls are small-bodied and long-legged. The birds can usually be spotted standing on the ground or on fenceposts. TOM TIETZ

67 | PURGATOIRE RIVER STATE WILDLIFE AREA

Description: An area of sagebrush-covered sandhills, interspersed with grasslands. The Purgatoire River runs through the state wildlife area. Several seasonal canals and ponds result in marshy areas. Cottonwood riparian communities along the river, with scattered tamarisk and Russian olive.

Viewing Information: Watch for beaver sign around ponds; beavers may be seen at dusk and dawn. Good waterfowl viewing year round. Mallards and wood ducks nesting; other ducks include pintails, gadwalls, wigeons, three teal species, and an occasional canvasback. Raptor viewing is especially good, in winter, for red-tailed, Swainson's, rough-legged, and ferruginous hawks, northern harriers, kestrels, and occasional bald and golden eagles. Great blue herons use the river and ponds, and sandhill cranes stop during migration. Watch for wild turkeys, pheasants, and bobwhite and scaled quail. Numerous songbirds, especially grassland species such as meadowlarks and lark buntings. Mammals include deer, red foxes, coyotes, and fox squirrels. You may see sign of weasels, bobcats, and raccoons.

Ownership: CDOW (719-336-4852)
Size: 950 acres
Closest Town: Las Animas
Directions: See map below

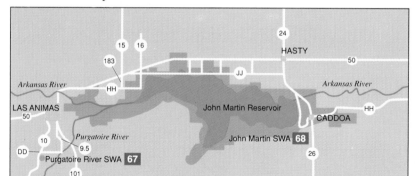

 Look for the many signs that animals have been present. Watch for tracks, dens, scratches, signs of a kill, scat (feces), and other giveaways.

68 JOHN MARTIN RESERVOIR STATE WIDLIFE AREA

Description: Distinct habitats comprise this state wildlife area. The north shore is rolling shortgrass prairie with bluffs overlooking the lake. The west end, where the Arkansas River feeds the reservoir, is marshy with small ponds. There is a large riparian community along Rule Creek on the south.

Viewing Information: The entire north shore is a huge prairie dog colony. Burrowing owls, jackrabbits, bullsnakes, and rattlesnakes inhabit prairie dog burrows. Attracted by the rodents, many predators may be seen in the vicinity including golden eagles, coyotes, badgers, and ferruginous, Swainson's, and red-tailed hawks. Lots of turkey vultures visible early April through late September. From December to February golden eagles and bald eagles use the area. Lots of waterfowl use the lake: wintering Canada geese and mallards, nesting wood ducks, and up to 100 white pelicans in summer. On the west end is an active cormorant/great blue heron colony of about 200 nests. Watch from afar March through July to avoid disturbing the birds. Numerous songbirds are found in the cottonwood stands; active beaver ponds on the west side. Watch for high concentrations of wildlife—songbirds, shorebirds, white pelicans, pheasant, bobwhite and scaled quail, wild turkeys, and deer—in a two-mile section along Rule Creek. Lots of coyotes—watch for them on the ice in winter.

Ownership: BOR, CDOW (719-336-4852)
Size: 22,000 acres
Closest Town: Las Animas
Directions: See map opposite page

Black-tailed prairie dogs live in large colonies, or towns, on Colorado's eastern plains. Prairie dog towns are a complex series of interconnected tunnels with more than one entrance.

MICHAEL S. SAMPLE

85

69 WILLOW CREEK PARK

Description: This municipal park in the city of Lamar of the best places in the state to see nesting Mississippi kites.

Viewing Information: Mississippi kites arrive in early April, nesting in trees throughout the park. Watch for them flying around the park feeding on flying insects, particularly cicadas. The range of these graceful raptors is expanding. They were first found nesting in Colorado only thirty years ago. Kites leave the area by the end of August.

Ownership: City of Lamar
(719-336-4601)
Size: Four square blocks
Closest Town: Lamar
Directions: See map this page

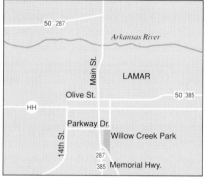

Mississippi kites are an uncommon sight in Colorado. Using their talons, kites catch and eat large insects in the air and grab small rodents and snakes on the ground. CATHY AND GORDON ILLG

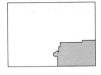

Description: This state wildlife area encompasses several large, open reservoirs—Nee Noshe, Nee Gronda, Nee So Pah, and Upper and Lower Queens—surrounded by agricultural fields and shortgrass prairie. Thin bands of cottonwoods grow along high water marks and there are sandy and muddy shores in low-water areas. Water levels fluctuate substantially due to irrigation needs. Bird species vary by water level fluctuation.

Viewing Information: Excellent for shore and wading birds in low water years—phalaropes, avocets, sandpipers, black-necked stilts, and dowitchers. Piping plovers, a threatened species, and endangered least terns have nested here in recent years. Observe the signs denoting sensitive wildlife nesting areas along the beach. Also snowy plovers and large accumulations of white pelicans. Snow geese numbers impressive in late February and early March in high water years. Variety of dabbling and diving ducks; also western, Clark's, eared, pied-billed, and horned grebes. Occasional longspurs among flocks of horned larks in upland areas in winter and spring.

Ownership: PVT, BLM, CDOW
(719-473-2945)
Size: 4,426 acres
Closest Town: Eads
Directions: See map this page

Typically seen wading in shallow water, the American avocet is characterized by its thin upturned bill. The avocet's unique black-and-white wings also make it readily identifiable in flight or from a distance.

D. ROBERT FRANZ

71 TWO BUTTES STATE WILDLIFE AREA

Description: Shortgrass prairie and old agricultural fields surround a reservoir that is often dry. Cottonwood riparian zones above and below the reservoir, expanding into dry lake bed. A spring below the dam feeds a marshy area. The creek leads into a prairie canyon with Native American petroglyphs on the rocky walls.

Viewing Information: Good site to view white-tailed and mule deer, pronghorn, cottontails, prairie dogs, and other small mammals. Wild turkeys in morning and evening, also pheasants and scaled quail. As many as 200 turkey vultures roost in cottonwoods at the west end of the property. If the wind is right, golden eagles congregate, using thermals off the buttes. Good fall hawk migration site, with kettles of up to 100 Swainson's hawks. In spring the area below the dam is very good for marsh birds and riparian songbirds—warblers, indigo buntings, blue grosbeaks, brown thrashers, and northern orioles. Good spot for plains, spadefoot, and red-spotted toads, painted and box turtles, collared and fence lizards, and various snakes.

Ownership: CDOW (719-336-4852)
Size: 4,962 acres
Closest Town: Springfield
Directions: See map this page

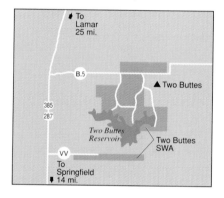

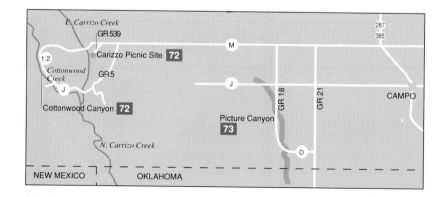

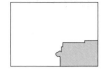

72 CARRIZO PICNIC SITE/COTTON-WOOD CANYON

Description: Carrizo and Cottonwood canyons are prairie canyons surrounded by sagebrush uplands dotted with pinyon/juniper. Rocky terrain on canyon tops with cottonwood riparian areas at the bottom. Access Carrizo Canyon at the picnic site and walk into the canyon. Brands hanging from a cable denote the start of private property. A county road winds through Cottonwood Canyon, but adjacent lands are private.

Viewing Information: Excellent spring birding for eastern phoebes, wild turkeys, roadrunners, scaled quail, pinyon jays, kingbirds, cliff swallows, mockingbirds, nighthawks, woodpeckers, and hummingbirds. Also Bewick's, rock, and canyon wrens. Turkey vultures common. Excellent raptor site, including nesting hawks, golden eagles and falcons. Burrowing owls in upland areas. Various toads and frogs around streamside pools. Watch for collared, fence, and western horned lizards. Coachwhips, western hognose snakes, western rattlesnakes and bullsnakes also common. A herd of bighorn sheep inhabits Cottonwood Canyon, with best viewing late fall and winter. Tarantulas highly visible migrating in fall.

Ownership: USFS (719-523-6591)
Size: 1,320 acres
Closest Town: Campo
Directions: See map opposite page

73 PICTURE CANYON

Description: Picture Canyon is named for the Native American pictographs and petroglyphs on its walls. An open, sloping canyon with shortgrass prairie and shrublands on top. Take a 1.5-mile drive into the canyon, accessible by car in dry weather, then a .5-mile walk into the rock art area.

Viewing Information: Excellent site for semi-desert grassland birds. Golden eagles nest here. Other raptors including prairie falcons, kestrels, turkey vultures, and a variety of hawks. Deer, bats, rabbits, and many small mammals. Rattlesnakes are seen, as well as painted and box turtles.

Ownership: USFS (719-523-6591)
Size: 1.5-mile drive, .5-mile walk
Closest Town: Campo
Directions: See map opposite page

74 LESSER PRAIRIE-CHICKEN LEK

Description: The ancestral lek, or booming ground, is an open area on the shortgrass prairie of the Comanche National Grassland. The best time for viewing is from about one half hour before sunrise until about 9 a.m. Dancing occurs from early March through mid-May, with peak activity in April when the hens arrive. Arrive at the lek well before dawn. If the blind is unavailable, remain in your car to avoid flushing the birds. The birds also display in the evening, but not as dramatically. Binoculars or spotting scopes are recommended.

Viewing Information: The males' courtship display, meant to attract females, involves bowing, drooping the wings, raising the antennae-like feathers on the head, drumming the feet, pirouetting, and sparring with rival males. The "booming" is made when the birds expel air from brightly colored air sacs on their throats.

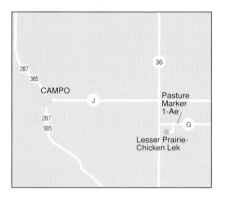

Ownership: USFS (719-523-6591)
Size: N/A
Closest Town: Campo
Directions: See map this page

Arrive before daybreak to see the dance of the lesser prairie-chickens. These rarely seen birds return to the lek each spring to take part in this fascinating mating spectacle.

JUDD COONEY

SOUTH CENTRAL REGION

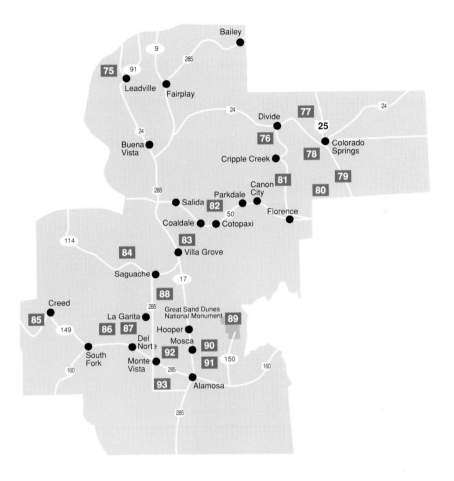

SITE 75	MOUNT ZION WINTERING ELK SITE
SITE 76	MUELLER STATE PARK
SITE 77	SANTA FE TRAIL, AIR FORCE ACADEMY
SITE 78	BEAR CREEK CANYON REGIONAL PARK
SITE 79	COLORADO SPRINGS STATE WILDLIFE AREA
SITE 80	FORT CARSON
SITE 81	PHANTOM CANYON ON THE GOLD BELT TOUR
SITE 82	BIGHORN SHEEP CANYON
SITE 83	HAYDEN PASS
SITE 84	TRICKLE MOUNTAIN

SITE 85	SILVER THREAD SCENIC BYWAY
SITE 86	NATURAL ARCH
SITE 87	LA GARITA CREEK RIPARIAN DEMONSTRATION AREA
SITE 88	RUSSELL LAKES STATE WILDLIFE AREA
SITE 89	GREAT SAND DUNES NATIONAL MONUMENT
SITE 90	SAN LUIS LAKES STATE WILDLIFE AREA
SITE 91	BLANCA WILDLIFE HABITAT AREA
SITE 92	RIO GRANDE STATE WILDLIFE AREA
SITE 93	MONTE VISTA NATIONAL WILDLIFE REFUGE

75 | MOUNT ZION WINTERING ELK SITE

Description: Pullouts along U.S. 24 and CO 91 offer viewing of elk on a rancher's pasture and feeding lot; the elk are drawn to natural and human-provided food sources. Use caution when stopping; the highway is narrow and visibility poor. Binoculars are necessary for highway viewing.

Viewing Information: Up to forty elk are visible feeding early in the morning and in the evening. Additional viewing along U.S. 24 of elk feeding on the south-facing slopes of Mount Zion.

Ownership: USFS, PVT, BLM
(719-275-0631)
Size: Five acres
Closest Town: Leadville
Directions: See map this page

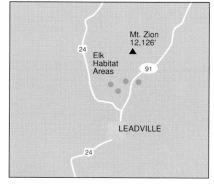

Aspen groves create an open canopy which enables sunlight to penetrate to the forest floor and encourage extensive plant growth. The diverse plant life in these groves provides food and shelter for hundreds of wildlife species, including elk.

SHERM SPOELSTRA

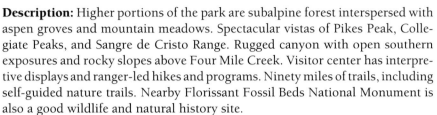

Description: Higher portions of the park are subalpine forest interspersed with aspen groves and mountain meadows. Spectacular vistas of Pikes Peak, Collegiate Peaks, and Sangre de Cristo Range. Rugged canyon with open southern exposures and rocky slopes above Four Mile Creek. Visitor center has interpretive displays and ranger-led hikes and programs. Ninety miles of trails, including self-guided nature trails. Nearby Florissant Fossil Beds National Monument is also a good wildlife and natural history site.

Viewing Information: Golden eagles nest on Dome Rock. Active beaver colony along Four Mile Creek. Watch for elk in meadows. Good winter viewing of bighorn sheep along Four Mile Creek. Listen and look in the high mountain forest for subalpine birds, such as blue grouse, crossbills, Cassin's finches, pine grosbeaks, and hermit thrushes. Small mammals include chickarees, chipmunks, and weasels.

Ownership: CDOW, CDPOR (719-687-2366)
Size: 12,103 acres
Closest Town: Divide
Directions: See map this page

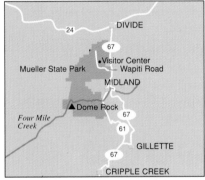

Long-tailed weasels are voracious predators. Their brown coat in summer and white coat in winter help camouflage them as they prey on small mammals.
DENNIS AND MARIA HENRY

93

77 SANTA FE TRAIL, AIR FORCE ACADEMY

Description: This eight-mile compacted gravel trail follows Monument Creek the entire length of the academy property. The corridor traverses a transition zone with cottonwood/alder riparian habitat along the creek on one side, and ponderosa pine/scrub oak foothills community on the other. The path is open to foot, horse, and mountain bike traffic. No parking allowed at trail access points on Academy grounds; parking is available on Baptist Road. Good wildlife viewing from the car through the rest of the academy. Stop at the visitor center upon entering the grounds.

Viewing Information: Excellent opportunity to see mule and white-tailed deer throughout the grounds. You may see elk and pronghorn in this transition area. Good grassland, riparian, and shrubland songbird viewing in spring and summer. Look and listen for hummingbirds in the foothills. Peregrine falcons have nested in the site; watch also for golden eagles, northern harriers, turkey vultures, and various grassland hawks. Good chance of seeing wild turkeys in morning or evening.

Ownership: US Air Force
(719-472-2025)
Size: Eight miles one way
Closest Town: Colorado Springs
Directions: See map this page

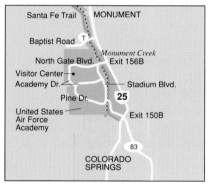

Western bluebirds of the southern Rockies are distinguished from other western bluebirds by a rust-colored breast and back.
R. E. BARBER

Description: The park combines foothills terrain dotted with Gambel oak thickets, areas of open meadows with yucca and native grasses, and cottonwood riparian zones along an intermittent creek. There are hiking trails, an equestrian center, playgrounds, tennis courts, and sports fields. The nature center has interpretive and live animal displays, self-guided nature trails, interpretive programs, and naturalists on duty.

Viewing Information: Mule deer live in the park. Watch also for cottontails, rock squirrels, and other meadow rodents. Red foxes and coyotes may be visible. Watch for signs of raccoons, short-tailed weasels, and bear (especially in fall). Sharp-shinned, Cooper's, and goshawks in wooded areas. Rufous-sided towhees and scrub jays abound. Watch for five races of dark-eyed junco. Warblers include yellow-rumped, MacGillivray's, Virginia's, and Wilson's. Western tanagers are abundant in spring, pine siskins in winter. Nesting broad-tailed hummingbirds. Other birds include great horned owls, meadowlarks, goldfinches, northern orioles, brown creepers, black-capped and mountain chickadees, and white crowned sparrows. In warm months watch for Woodhouse's toads, box turtles, hognose and garter snakes, and bullsnakes.

Ownership: El Paso County (719-520-6387)
Size: 1,235 acres
Closest Town: Colorado Springs
Directions: See map this page

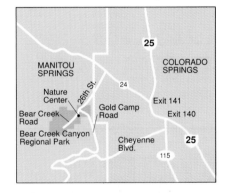

The great horned owl is known for its large size and long ear tufts. Its wing feather design enables this nocturnal hunter to fly silently through the woods.

SHERM SPOELSTRA

79 COLORADO SPRINGS STATE WILDLIFE AREA

Description: The property straddles Interstate 25 with access at three highway exits. A 1.75-mile nature trail with boardwalks leads through cottonwood riparian habitat along Fountain Creek. West of I-25 is shortgrass prairie with yucca and cholla cactus. Cultivated fields provide agricultural habitat and wildlife forage.

Viewing Information: More than 200 wildlife species have been recorded here. Watch for rufous-sided towhees, blue grosbeaks, swallows, kingbirds, lazuli buntings, and many other songbirds. "Woodpecker Meadow" has been nick-named for the five species of woodpecker seen there. Numerous shore, marsh, and wading birds: great blue herons, white-faced ibis, yellowlegs, killdeer, and common snipe. Many migrant waterfowl. Raptors such as red-tailed, Swainson's, rough-legged, and ferruginous hawks. Mammals include coyotes, red foxes, raccoons, skunks, deer, and rabbits.

Ownership: CDOW (719-382-5060)
Size: 3,900 acres
Closest Town: Fountain
Directions: See map this page

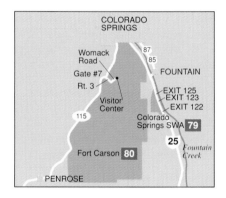

80 FORT CARSON

Description: A large, diverse viewing site with ponds, grasslands, montane shrublands, pinyon/juniper woodlands, and cottonwood riparian habitat. Per-mit is necessary for wildlife viewing on Fort Carson. Stop at the visitor center before proceeding.

Viewing Information: Watch for coots, grebes, mallards, mergansers, and other waterbirds. Good raptor viewing includes golden eagles, prairie falcons, and hawks. Wooded areas attract a variety of songbirds. Mammals include prairie dogs, rabbits, a unique plains elk herd, pronghorn, and mule deer. Inquire at the visitor center for specific viewing information.

Ownership: US Army (719-579-2752)
Size: 130,000 acres
Closest Town: Colorado Springs
Directions: See map above

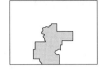

81 PHANTOM CANYON ON THE GOLD BELT TOUR

Description: This rocky canyon on the Gold Belt Tour follows Eight Mile Creek along the former bed of the Florence and Cripple Creek Railroad, once a lifeline to the gold camps. The route starts in arid areas of native grasses and cholla cactus. Lower reaches of the canyon reveal pinyon/juniper-covered slopes with cottonwoods along the water. Upper reaches of the canyon feature Engelmann spruce and subalpine fir with patches of aspen. The road is gravel, one-lane in places, and portions are confined by narrow canyon walls. Do not attempt to drive it with travel trailers, motor homes, or large campers.

Viewing Information: Watch for roadrunners in the canyon's lower end and numerous songbirds among riparian areas. Canyon species include canyon wrens, mountain bluebirds, swifts, and swallows. Watch for blue grouse in higher-elevation forests and wild turkeys feeding near the creek early and late in the day. Cliff-nesting raptors include golden eagles, red-tailed hawks, and prairie falcons. Peregrine falcons nest in a side canyon near the Beaver Creek Wilderness Study Area. Watch for mule deer in open areas.

Ownership: PVT, BLM
(719-275-0631)
Size: Fifteen miles one-way
Closest Town: Cripple Creek/Florence
Directions: See map this page

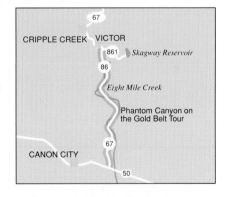

CRIPPLE CREEK   VICTOR
67
861   Skagway Reservoir
86
Eight Mile Creek
Phantom Canyon on
the Gold Belt Tour
67
CANON CITY
50

One of six almost identical small flycatchers that nest in Colorado, the willow flycatcher favors large expanses of willows along high country streams. Despite their physical similarities, all species nest in different habitats and have a different song.
GEORGE H. H. HUEY

82 BIGHORN SHEEP CANYON

Description: A developed interpretive facility at the Five Points Recreation Site offers information about bighorn sheep and other wildlife. Bighorn sheep are frequently visible at the recreation area. Watchable Wildlife signs throughout the canyon draw attention to other likely bighorn sheep viewing points between Parkdale and Salida. The canyon is rocky and narrow, with steep cliffs and pinyon/juniper woodlands. Scenic views along the Arkansas River. Use caution and watch for other traffic when viewing the bighorn sheep.

Viewing Information: Bighorn sheep are visible on both north and south-facing slopes of the canyon right along the highway. Best viewing is from Coaldale to Parkdale as the bighorn sheep come down to the river to drink. Bighorn sheep can be seen year round, but winter viewing is best.

Ownership: BLM (719-275-0631)
Size: Forty-five-mile drive
Closest Town: Canon City, Parkdale, Salida
Directions: See map this page

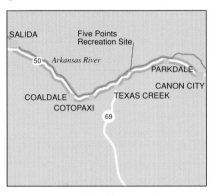

Colorado's state mammal, the Rocky Mountain bighorn sheep is easily observed, but blends well into its habitat. Look for its familiar white rump patch. The male's antlers curl downward and the female's are spike-like. DONALD M. JONES

83 ▌ HAYDEN PASS

Description: A four-wheel-drive route from Villa Grove to Coaldale, cresting the 11,184-foot summit of Hayden Pass with spectacular views of the Wet Mountain Valley to the east and the San Luis Valley to the west. Route passes through a variety of landscapes, from sagebrush and meadowlands through oakbrush, and pinyon/juniper, to ponderosa pine and spruce/fir forests.

Viewing Information: Pronghorn are almost always visible in uplands. Elk and deer can be seen in higher-elevation open areas. Bald eagles are occasionally sighted. Watch for ravens, gray and Steller's jays, and a variety of woodland and grassland hawks.

Ownership: PVT, BLM, USFS
(719-655-2547)
Size: Fifteen miles one-way
Closest Town: Villa Grove/Coaldale
Directions: See map this page

The road across Hayden Pass traverses pinyon/juniper terrain, summer home of the black-chinned hummingbird. This hummingbird is feeding on Indian paint-brush nectar. CLAUDE STEELMAN

99

TRICKLE MOUNTAIN

Description: A mosaic of open grasslands with Douglas fir and ponderosa pine in draws and arroyos. Some aspen stands, with mountain shrubs on hillsides. Riparian zones of alder. Fairly sheer cliffs on the south and southwest offer good raptor nesting. Good road system. Currently no foot trails, though interpretive trails are planned. County road access is by four-wheel-drive vehicle only. Restrictions prohibit vehicle use from March 15 to May 15 due to wet conditions.

Viewing Information: Trickle Mountain features Colorado's four major hoofed species—pronghorn, mule deer, elk, and bighorn sheep—all using the same habitat. Golden eagles and prairie falcons nest in cliffs. Rough-legged hawks frequent the area and peregrine falcons are occasionally sighted. Management site for Rio Grande cutthroat trout. Look for beaver ponds on Tuttle Creek.

Ownership: BLM (719-589-4975)
Size: 53,000 acres
Closest Town: Saguache
Directions: See map this page

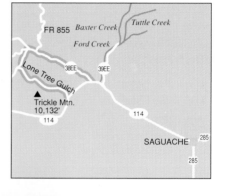

This mule deer buck will shed its antlers in the winter and begin growing another set in the spring. The animal was named for its large, mulelike ears.

DENNIS HENRY

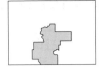

Description: An outstanding seventy-five-mile scenic drive from South Fork to Lake City, via Creede. Route passes through mountain meadows, riverine mountain riparian areas along the Rio Grande River, and subalpine forest of spruce/fir and aspen. Crossing the Continental Divide at Spring Creek Pass, the route winds over Slumgullion Pass into Lake City. Outstanding vistas, with good views of alpine regions, cascading waterfalls, geological formations, and historical and cultural sites.

Viewing Information: Moose were released between the Hinsdale County line and north to Spring Creek Pass in 1991 and 1992; watch for them in willow bottoms. In winter look for elk at dawn and dusk at the Coller State Wildlife Area. Deer might be seen anywhere year-round. Bighorn sheep are often visible from the highway on cliffs and south-facing slopes, especially fall and winter. Best spots are Blue Creek to Wagon Wheel Gap and Seepage Creek to Clear Creek. Bald eagles are seen along the Rio Grande in winter. In summer watch for golden eagles, goshawks, red-tailed hawks, ravens, coyotes, and marmots. Subalpine forests offer good summertime songbird viewing.

Ownership: CDOW, PVT, USFS, BLM (719-658-2556/303-641-0471)
Size: Seventy-five miles
Closest Town: South Fork/Creede/ Lake City
Directions: See map this page

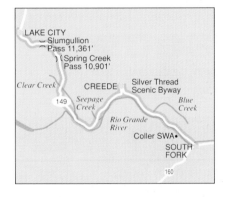

LAKE CITY
Slumgullion Pass 11,361'
Spring Creek Pass 10,901'
Clear Creek   CREEDE   Silver Thread Scenic Byway
149   Seepage Creek   Blue Creek
Rio Grande River
Coller SWA•
SOUTH FORK
160

Moose were reintroduced to Colorado in the late 1970s, and their range is expanding. Wet areas dominated by willows and adjacent to coniferous forests make ideal moose habitat.

DENNIS HENRY

86 | NATURAL ARCH

Description: Located within the Summer Cone Volcano, the Natural Arch is a wall of volcanic rock with a window through it. Surrounding terrain combines rolling pinyon/juniper woodlands with open grasslands. From the picnic area at the end of the road a 1.5-hour hike leads further into bighorn sheep country. Request the "Animal Lovers" brochure on area wildlife watching from the USFS office in Del Norte.

Viewing Information: Look for bighorn sheep in the vicinity of the Natural Arch Picnic Ground on dry, south-facing slopes and rock faces. Watch for pronghorn as you drive into the area. Elk are visible in winter; deer, bighorn sheep, and pronghorn can be seen year-round.

Ownership: BLM, PVT, USFS (719-657-3321)
Size: 100 acres
Closest Town: Del Norte
Directions: See map this page

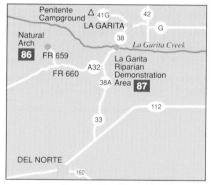

Long ears, long legs, and a preference for dry grassland and shrub habitats differenti-
102   *ate this jackrabbit from its relative, the cottontail.* SHERM SPOELSTRA

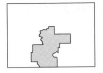

87 LA GARITA CREEK RIPERIAN DEMONSTRATION AREA

Description: Cottonwood/alder/willow riparian zones along the creek surrounded by wet meadows and pastureland. Located where the creek flows out of the mountains onto the valley floor. The area is being managed to improve water quality and fish habitat, stabilize banks, and improve riparian vegetation to serve as an example of what can be done to manage riparian sites.

Viewing Information: An excellent area for viewing migratory and nesting songbirds: orioles, thrushes, towhees, vireos, wrens, warblers, chickadees, sparrows, woodpeckers, and juncos. Good site for great horned owls. Great blue herons use sandy flats along the creek. Elk, mule deer, and pronghorn can be sighted along CO 112 and County Road 33 to La Garita.

Ownership: BLM (719-589-4975)
Size: 1,375 acres
Closest Town: Del Norte
Directions: See map opposite page

Dark-eyed juncos forage on the ground for seeds and insects. The birds often nest in small, well-concealed ground impressions. WELDON LEE

Water attracts many varieties of birds to the Russell Lakes State Wildlife Area in southern Colorado's San Luis Valley. BOB HERNBRODE

Description: Large wetland complex with many marshes and small, shallow lakes providing excellent habitat for migratory waterfowl, wading birds, and shorebirds. Located among dry shrublands of the San Luis Valley. Portions are closed to public access during waterfowl and shorebird nesting periods, April 15 to July 15. Binoculars are necessary. Winter viewing opportunities are limited. Interpretive signs, trails, and boardwalks are planned.

Viewing Information: Because the water source is primarily artesian wells, viewing opportunities are nearly year-round for waterfowl, wading birds, and shorebirds. Excellent opportunities to see white-faced ibis, snowy egrets, and white pelicans, as well as a wide variety of songbirds. Nesting avocets, spotted sandpipers, Wilson's phalaropes, and black terns. Watch for shorebirds in ditches along the county roads.

Ownership: BOR, CDOW
(719-852-4783)
Size: 5,433 acres
Closest Town: Saguache
Directions: See map this page

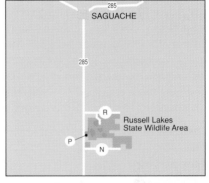

This female Wilson's phalarope is more colorful and larger than her mate. The birds spin top-like in the water and feed on insects sucked into the resulting whirlpool. KEN ARCHER

105

89 GREAT SAND DUNES NATIONAL MONUMENT

Description: The national monument is a fascinating geological site with sand dunes up to 700 feet high at the base of the Sangre de Cristo Range. Lacking vegetation, the dunes themselves have little animal life. Surrounding habitats include currant/rabbitbrush shrublands, and pinyon/juniper woodlands. Scattered ponderosa pine, a few aspen groves and cottonwood riparian areas border Medano and Mosca creeks, as well as other intermittent waterways through the monument. Inquire at the visitor center for information. There is a half-mile nature trail and guided nature walks.

Viewing Information: Mule deer are visible everywhere, and elk are sometimes seen in winter near the entrance. Pronghorn can be seen on the approach to the monument, and bighorn sheep are visible along the road to Medano Pass (requires four-wheel-drive vehicle). Kangaroo rats are everywhere at night; watch for their holes in vegetated upland areas. Other mammals include chipmunks, rock and golden-mantled ground squirrels, desert and Nuttall's cottontails, coyotes, and bobcats. Animal tracks are visible on the dunes in early morning. Good songbird viewing in wooded areas. Species include magpies, scrub, pinyon, and Steller's jays, mountain bluebirds, chickadees, flickers, Lewis' and downy woodpeckers, nutcrackers, grosbeaks, broad-tailed and rufous hummingbirds, white-throated swifts, green-tailed towhees, and nighthawks.

Ownership: NPS (719-378-2312)
Size: 38,659 acres
Closest Town: Mosca
Directions: See map below

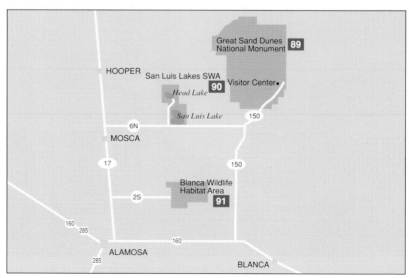

90 SAN LUIS LAKES STATE WILDLIFE AREA

Description: Shrubland of salt grass, greasewood, and rabbitbrush surrounds Head and San Luis lakes. Sedge/bulrush wet meadows in low-lying areas between the lakes. The area is fed by intermittent water from springs and San Luis Creek; very wet during spring runoff. The southern one-third of the area is under development as a state park. Portions are closed to public access during waterfowl and shorebird nesting periods, February 15 to July 15.

Viewing Information: Many resident Canada geese and dabbling ducks, especially mallards, pintails, and gadwalls. Good potential for seeing concentrations of canvasbacks and occasional mergansers on San Luis Lake. Also white pelicans and herons on the lakes; bitterns, snipe, and snowy plovers in the meadows.

Ownership: CDOW, CDPOR
Size: 2,054 acres
Closest Town: Mosca
Directions: See map opposite page

91 BLANCA WILDLIFE HABITAT AREA

Description: Large acreage on the floor of the San Luis Valley below 14,345-foot Blanca Peak consists of old lake beds edged by sand dunes. Earthen dikes and artesian wells have created a series of ponds as waterfowl nesting habitat. Some ponds have cattail/bulrush marshes; others offer wild plum, Russian olive, and cottonwoods to encourage various wildlife species. Portions are closed to public access during waterfowl and shorebird nesting periods, February 15 to July 15. Biting insects are severe in July and August. Interpretive trails are planned and a portion of the area may be opened year-round for viewing access.

Viewing Information: Excellent duck viewing. Shore, wading, and marsh birds include avocets, black-crowned night-herons, several species of sandpipers, and red-winged and yellow-headed blackbirds. Waterflow designed to keep some ponds ice-free in winter, attracting bald eagles. BLM has erected eagle roosts. Good viewing hawks, as well as northern harriers. Mammals include muskrats, cottontails, foxes, and coyotes.

Ownership: BLM (719-589-4975)
Size: 7,125 acres
Closest Town: Alamosa
Directions: See map opposite page

92 RIO GRANDE STATE WILDLIFE AREA

Description: An area of developed ponds and wetlands managed for waterfowl along the Rio Grande River. Thick cottonwood/willow communities in bottomlands along the river channel. Artesian wells feed warmwater ponds surrounded by scattered cottonwoods. Area closed to public access during waterfowl and shorebird nesting, February 15 to July 15.

Viewing Information: Excellent viewing of resident waterfowl. Many dabbling ducks (mallards, gadwalls, pintails) and Canada geese. Look for diving ducks on the bigger ponds, especially ruddy ducks and goldeneyes. Some sandhill cranes in spring and fall. Occasional great blue herons, night-herons, white-faced ibis, and bitterns in marshy areas. Good area for cavity-nesting songbirds in wooded areas—swallows, woodpeckers, and creepers—and warblers among the willows. Raptors include great horned owls, northern harriers, Swainson's and ferruginous hawks, and bald eagles (in winter). Numerous beavers, muskrats, and mule deer.

Ownership: CDOW (719-852-4783)
Size: 1,450 acres
Closest Town: Monte Vista
Directions: See map this page

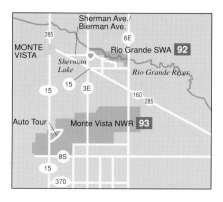

Wild ducks usually have special habitat requirements. Dabbling ducks, like mallards and teal, prefer shallow marshes and small potholes, where they bob tail-up for food. Diving ducks, such as redheads and scaup, congregate at deeper bodies of water, where they readily dive to feed.

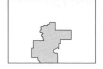

93 | MONTE VISTA NATIONAL WILDLIFE REFUGE

Description: Located in the arid San Luis Valley, the refuge is a complex of ponds and marshes created and managed to provide nesting and feeding habitat for waterfowl and other wildlife. By contrast, surrounding greasewood uplands are dry. Farmed plots of grain and alfalfa supplement natural food sources.

Viewing Information: Throughout March the refuge and surrounding fields are an important staging ground for greater sandhill cranes. Look for a few whooping cranes in the sandhill flock. Thousands of cranes return in October and stay four to eight weeks. Twenty species of ducks and four species of geese have been sighted here along with swans, snipe, sandpipers, herons, egrets, and numerous songbirds. Fall duck populations can exceed 35,000. Bald eagles visible in winter. A bird list is available. Mammals include mule deer, muskrats, rabbits, and coyotes. The self-guided auto tour route is open dawn to dusk year round. Headquarters is Alamosa National Wildlife Refuge, also worth a visit. It is located southeast of Alamosa along the Rio Grande.

Ownership: USFWS (719-589-4021)
Size: 14,189 acres
Closest Town: Monte Vista
Directions: See map opposite page

During spring and fall migrations, endangered whooping cranes stop over at Monte Vista National Wildlife Refuge in the San Luis Valley. The whoopers travel with flocks of sandhill cranes. D. ROBERT FRANZ

Fairly common yet rarely seen, mountain lions stake out large territories often encompassing many square miles. There, the secretive cats hunt deer, their dietary staple. JUDD COONEY

SOUTHWEST REGION

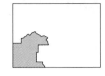

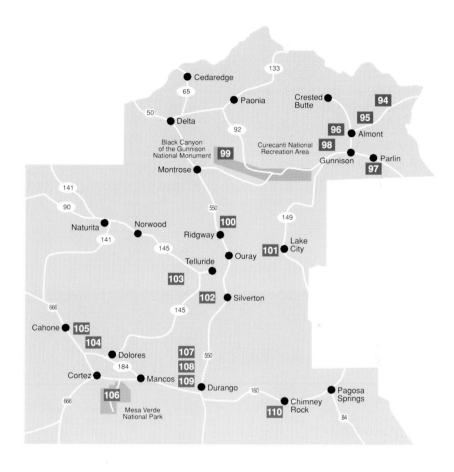

94 | TAYLOR RIVER BRIDGE

Description: The bridge overlooks a series of pools in the Taylor River just below Taylor Park Reservoir. Interpretive signs and a handicapped-accessible fishing pier are planned. Just above the bridge is a viewing site with interpretive information on the dam and spillway.

Viewing Information: Excellent opportunity to view large brown and rainbow trout in the river. Fish can be seen best with polarized glasses. In winter you may see bald eagles along the river on the drive through Taylor Canyon.

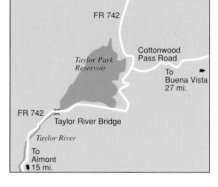

Ownership: USFS (303-641-0471)
Size: .5-mile of river
Closest Town: Almont
Directions: See map this page

Rainbow trout are raised in Colorado fish hatcheries and released into state rivers and lakes to supplement native fisheries. KEN ARCHER

Description: The "triangle" is bordered by the Taylor and East rivers and County/Forest Road 813. It is a sagebrush, aspen, and mixed conifer wintering range for bighorn sheep, mule deer, and elk. Prime viewing areas are marked by signs and parking.

Viewing Information: From late November through April, watch for bighorn sheep on south- and east-facing slopes on the southern edge of the triangle and in the Taylor River Canyon. Deer are most visible along the East River, with elk sighted everywhere. To protect the animals, the area is closed to public access December 1 through April 1, when viewing must be done from the highway. Some bighorn sheep are visible in summer.

Ownership: City of Gunnison, USFS (303-641-0471)
Size: Twenty-five square miles
Closest Town: Almont
Directions: See map this page

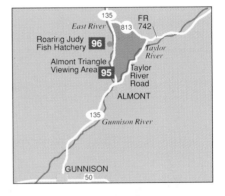

Description: The hatchery is located in a wide valley along the East River. Sagebrush hillsides above low-lying grassy meadows with willow thickets and cottonwood riparian areas along the river. Numerous springs provide year-round water. The hatchery is open seven days a week from 8 a.m. to 4:30 p.m.

Viewing Information: Lots of shore and songbirds in the marshy willow bottoms and wet meadows. In winter, watch for bald eagles along the river. Osprey are occasionally sighted. Kokanee salmon are spawned in the hatchery from late October to early November. Visitors can view the milking and fertilization of eggs. Call the hatchery for viewing times. Young salmon, cutthroat, and rainbow trout can be viewed in ponds and raceways at the hatchery.

Ownership: CDOW (303-641-0190
Size: 776 acres
Closest Town: Almont
Directions: See map above

97 SOUTH PARLIN SAGE GROUSE SITE

Description: A low sagebrush flat with the lek in the center.

Viewing Information: From early April through mid-May, male sage grouse perform a courtship dance on an ancestral lek. The birds bend over, fan out their wings, raise and spread their tail feathers, and chase and jump at each other. They produce a popping sound by expelling air from their purple throat sacs. Best viewing time is just after dawn. Arrive at the lek before dawn so the birds don't see you. Cars act as a blind to which the birds pay little attention. Remain in your car while any birds are on the lek or they will flush.

Ownership: BLM (303-641-0471)
Size: Fifteen acres
Closest Town: Gunnison
Directions: See map below

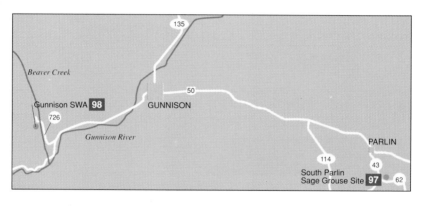

98 GUNNISON STATE WILDLIFE AREA

Description: Sagebrush hillsides surround irrigated hay meadows, with cotton-wood/willow riparian areas along the Beaver Creek drainage. The parking lot overlooks the valley bottom where elk and deer feed in winter. The CDOW is planting shrubs near the site to increase forage. There are interpretive signs at the overlook, and an interpretive trail to the creek is planned.

Viewing Information: The valley is important winter range for deer and elk. They are visible feeding in the meadow and on hillsides from late December to early March. In spring and summer songbird viewing along Beaver Creek is good.

Ownership: BLM, CDOW (303-641-0088)
Size: 2,800 acres
Closest Town: Gunnison
Directions: See map above

Description: Carved by the Gunnison River, this national monument features an awesome canyon with rocky walls rising over 2,000 feet in places. Much of the area is oak/serviceberry brushland, with some pinyon/juniper woodlands. Douglas-fir and some aspen are found in side canyons, with riparian vegetation along the river. Inquire at the visitor center for specific, up-to-date viewing opportunities.

Viewing Information: Hiking the Warner Point Trail is possibly the best way to see a variety of birds: ruby-crowned kinglets, mountain chickadees, western tanagers, hairy woodpeckers, Cooper's hawks, and an occasional golden eagle. Green-tailed towhees are common at the south rim campground, along with blue grouse and various nesting warblers. Near East Portal, dippers can be seen along the river. Watch also for nesting yellow warblers, broad-tailed hummingbirds, and other songbirds. Doves, flickers, Steller's and scrub jays, and other birds are visible from the roads. From the overlooks watch for ravens, turkey vultures, white-throated swifts, violet-green swallows, and golden eagles. Bald eagles are common in winter. You may see endangered peregrine falcons which nest in the monument. Mule deer can be easily seen at dusk and early morning along both rims and in the campgrounds. Occasional elk, bighorn sheep, and black bears. Watch for numerous small mammals—chipmunks, ground squirrels, porcupines, marmots, rabbits, and skunks.

Ownership: NPS (303-249-7036)
Size: 20,766 acres
Closest Town: Montrose
Directions: See map this page

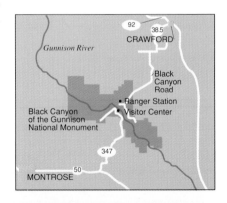

Nimble American dippers entertain wildlife viewers by plunging underwater into rushing streams while searching for insects. They bob and dip when standing on the shore. When airborne, these "water ouzels" fly close to the stream surface.
DENNIS HENRY

100 MONTROSE-OURAY DRIVE

Description: This scenic drive follows the Uncompahgre River through pinyon/juniper-dotted hillsides, cattle ranches, and alfalfa and hay fields. Cottonwood riparian zones occur along the river, and rugged, rocky cliffs near Ouray. Billy Creek State Wildlife Area and Ridgway State Park are along the route. Both are excellent deer and elk viewing sites. A partially paved bike path from Montrose to Ridgway Reservoir features interpretive signs and offers a good chance to view a variety of species.

Viewing Information: Mule deer are visible year-round all along the route. There is a chance of seeing bighorn sheep in the Ouray area. Elk can be seen in winter along the highway from Ridgway to Ouray. Watch for bald eagles along the river in winter; golden eagles and red-tailed and other hawks year-round. Sandhill cranes fly over the area in spring and fall; watch for them in fields along the highway. Watch for black swifts high over Ouray, at the head of Box Canyon and along the switchbacks of U.S. 550 south of Ouray. Look for prairie dogs, marmots, and coyotes in open areas. Many songbirds use the riparian zones along the river. Keep an eye open for great blue herons and other wading birds.

Ownership: PVT, CDOW, BLM, USFS (303-249-3711)
Size: Thirty-five-mile drive
Closest Town: Montrose, Ridgway, Ouray
Directions: See map this page

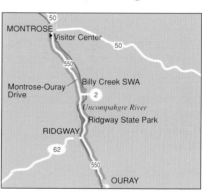

Red-tailed hawks have broad wings, an eerie and shrill cry, and a wide, rounded reddish tail. It's common to see the hawks being mobbed by smaller birds defending their territories and young.

JUDD COONEY

101 ALPINE LOOP

Description: This four-wheel-drive back country byway, much of it above timberline, offers good viewing of high alpine tundra and spectacular scenery of the rugged San Juan Mountains. From Lake City the route goes up the Lake Fork of the Gunnison River and over Cinnamon Pass. It passes the ghost town of Animas Forks with numerous old buildings still standing. Cresting Engineer Pass, the route follows Henson Creek back to Lake City. The loop, also accessible from Silverton and Ouray, traverses a variety of high country habitats—alpine zone above timberline, subalpine forests, open mountain meadows, and high mountain riparian zones. Several roadside pullouts have historical markers. Route is open late May or early June through late October.

Viewing Information: Watch for alpine dwellers such as ptarmigan, marmots, and pikas. Elk and deer may also be visible. Subalpine forests are home to blue grouse, chickarees, gray jays, Clark's nutcrackers, goshawks, and numerous other birds that find abundant food here in late summer. Watch for beaver dams along the Lake Fork of the Gunnison River and Henson Creek, and waterfowl on Lake San Cristobal.

Ownership: BLM (303-641-0471)
Size: Forty-five-mile loop drive
Closest Town: Lake City, Silverton, Ouray
Directions: See map this page

Visitors to the Alpine Loop Back Country Byway can hike to Sloan Lake on 14,048-foot Handies Peak. The trail leads 1.5 miles along Grizzly Gulch in the Handies Peak Wilderness Study Area.

JACK OLSON

102 PRIEST LAKES

Description: The Priest Lakes are located above 10,000 feet in spruce/fir and aspen forest interspersed with grassy meadows. Beaver ponds and willow/sedge riparian areas are found along the Lake Fork of the San Miguel River. Nearby Matterhorn Campground is located in a subalpine forest of Engelmann spruce and subalpine fir with patches of aspen. Trails lead into the Lizard Head Wilderness with good access to areas above timberline from nearby Lizard Head Pass. The site is located on the San Juan Skyway, CO 145.

Viewing Information: Watch for dabbling ducks and grebes. You may see buffleheads and goldeneyes. Elk and deer are occasionally visible. Active beaver colonies along the creek. Watch for songbirds among the willows and in the subalpine forest: warblers, nutcrackers, gray and Steller's jays, mountain chickadees, pine grosbeaks, red crossbills, and juncos. Forest raptors include Cooper's and sharp-shinned hawks. Also red-tailed hawks and golden eagles in open areas. Wetlands areas attract spotted sandpipers and killdeer.

Ownership: USFS (303-327-4261)
Size: Thirty acres
Closest Town: Telluride
Directions: See map this page

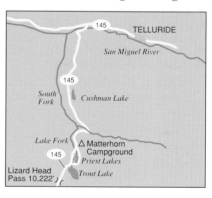

The pine grosbeak's heavy, crushing bill identifies it as a seed eater. Its two-note "chirrups" can often be heard by chairlift riders at Colorado ski resorts.

HARRY ENGELS

103 **WOODS LAKE**

Description: A high-altitude reservoir surrounded by spruce/fir forest, with some aspen and meadowland. A small willow community wetland is found where Fall Creek feeds into the lake. Four major trail systems access the Lizard Head Wilderness from the area. A very scenic site, with a backdrop of Flattop, Middle, and Dolores peaks, and the 14,000-foot summits of Mt. Wilson, Wilson Peak, and El Diente Peak to the southeast. The road from Beaver Park to Woods Lake is a scenic drive through subalpine forest.

Viewing Information: Look for an active beaver colony in the marshy area along Fall Creek. Watch for ducks—mallards, teal, an occasional bufflehead or merganser—on the lake or in the wetlands. Killdeer, sandpipers, and various shorebirds may be seen around the water's edge. Numerous woodland and riparian birds: downy and hairy woodpeckers, red-naped sapsuckers, gray jays, red crossbills, flickers, mountain bluebirds, various warblers, hummingbirds, and blue grouse. Woods Lake is a major elk calving site, so there's a good chance to view elk in June.

Ownership: CDOW, USFS
(303-327-4261)
Size: Sixty acres
Closest Town: Telluride
Directions: See map this page

NORWOOD 145
44Z
Lone Cone Road
62
San Miguel River
PLACERVILLE SAWPIT
M44 46M Fall Creek
44Z FR 611 FR 618 57P
FR 618 Woods
Beaver Park Lake

The green-winged teal's shiny green head patch makes it easily identifiable. A member of the duck family, the green-winged teal is half the size of the more common mallard.

CLAUDE STEELMAN

119

104 MCPHEE RESERVOIR

Description: A flooded river canyon with a sloping, timbered shore and several side canyons. McPhee is one of the largest reservoirs in the state. Shores are winter range for deer and elk. Surrounding slopes support pinyon/juniper and Douglas-fir woodlands with cultivated fields (some planted with alfalfa and grasses for wildlife forage). Surrounding wildlife management areas closed December 1 to March 31.

Viewing Information: Self-guided boat tour brochure highlights viewing opportunities along McPhee's fifty miles of shoreline. Numerous waterfowl and waterbirds on the lake. Canada geese, mergansers, coots, and a variety of ducks seen year-round. Look for mountain bluebirds, kingfishers, Steller's jays, rock squirrels, and muskrats. Wintering bald eagles and migrant osprey. An osprey nesting platform has been erected in hopes of attracting these "fishhawks" to nest. Predators include great horned owls, bobcats, and coyotes.

Ownership: BOR, USFS (303-882-7296)
Size: Fifty miles of shoreline.
Closest Town: Dolores
Directions: See map this page

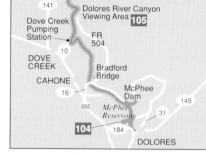

Redheads are diving ducks often confused with canvasbacks, whose heads are similarly colored. But the canvasback has a sloping head, while the redhead sports a distinctly round profile. DENNIS HENRY

105 DOLORES RIVER CANYON

Description: Dolores River Canyon offers excellent wildlife and scenery as well as hiking, mountain biking, four-wheeling, skiing, kayaking, canoeing, and other recreation. Ponderosa pine, pinyon/juniper habitat, and large meadows broken by riparian areas along the river. The canyon is 1,000-feet deep and fairly broad near the dam, becoming steep-sided at the lower end with up to twelve geologic layers visible. The first twelve miles of the road, from McPhee Dam to Bradfield Bridge, are passable by passenger car, though closed to motor vehicles December 1 through March 31 to protect wintering deer and elk. The next nineteen miles, from the bridge to Dove Creek Pumps, are passable only by foot or horseback after high water recedes (mid-June). The last twenty-eight miles, from the pumps to Slick Rock, are passable by four-wheel-drive the first thirteen miles; by foot, horse, and mountain bike the last fifteen miles.

Viewing Information: In spring watch for deer, elk, wild turkeys, and an array of meadow and woodland songbirds. River otters, endangered in Colorado, have been reintroduced to the Dolores. Watch for them in the river and along the bank. Bears and sign of bobcats and mountain lions may be seen in summer. Brown, rainbow, and Snake River cutthroat trout visible in pools. Bald eagles in winter, peregrine falcons in summer, and golden eagles are viewed year-round. Watch for wild turkeys moving to and from the river in morning and evening. A herd of desert bighorn sheep inhabits the steep lower section. Beaver dams and ponds along river.

Ownership: USFS, PVT, BOR, BLM
(303-247-4082)
Size: Fifty-five miles of river canyon
Closest Town: Dove Creek/Cahone/
Dolores
Directions: See map opposite page

Southwest Colorado's Dolores River Canyon offers wild country, ample recreational opportunities, and a strong sampling of the state's excellent wildlife viewing.

R. E. BARBER

106 MESA VERDE NATIONAL PARK

Description: The cliff dwellings of the Anasazi culture highlight this dramatic country of flat-topped mesas, steep canyons, and wonderful vistas. Mesa country terrain includes pinyon/juniper with scrub oak and fir in the draws, and sagebrush in open areas. Check at the visitor center for current viewing opportunities.

Viewing Information: The park's twisting canyons and rugged terrain offer good raptor viewing. Eagles, hawks, and vultures are visible soaring on thermal updrafts along the mesa's escarpment. The Knife Edge Trail has views of peregrine falcons and golden eagles, as well as red-tailed, Swainson's, Cooper's, and sharp-shinned hawks. Bald eagles and rough-legged hawks are seen in winter. The museum patio is a good place to watch hummingbirds. Mule deer are very common throughout the park. Prater Canyon is a good stop to view deer as well as wild turkeys. Spruce Tree Point features a turkey vulture roost. Look for ravens at Navajo Bend and Soda Canyon, and white-throated swifts at Cliff Palace Dwelling. Watch among the pines for scrub, pinyon, and Steller's jays. Carnivores sometimes seen along the park entrance road include coyotes, gray foxes, and an occasional black bear and mountain lion.

Ownership: NPS (303-529-4461)
Size: 52,000 acres
Closest Town: Cortez
Directions: See map this page

While justifiably famous for its ancient Anasazi Indian ruins, Mesa Verde National Park also provides wonderful wildlife viewing. This spectacular land of canyons and mesas is in the Four Corners region.
DAN PEHA

107 ANIMAS OVERLOOK INTERPRETIVE TRAIL

Description: Trail winds through mixed forest with views of the Animas River Valley. Interpretive stops explain the geology, forest ecology, wildlife, and human history of the site.

Viewing Information: Watch for eagles, turkey vultures, and several hawk species. Numerous songbirds. Jays, woodpeckers, red-naped sapsuckers, hummingbirds, ravens, and magpies are also found. Good place for chipmunks, ground squirrels, gray-phase Abert's squirrels, porcupines, and coyotes. Also elk, mule deer, and black bear. Reptiles include horned lizards, skinks, and various snakes.

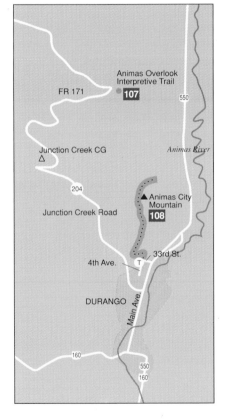

Ownership: USFS (303-247-4874)
Size: .7 mile
Closest Town: Durango
Directions: See map this page

108 ANIMAS CITY MOUNTAIN

Description: A rest stop for migrating birds. Interpretive nature trail loops 2.5 miles from the city limit around the top of this 8,400-foot mountain.

Viewing Information: Peregrine falcons can be observed hunting swallows on the cliffs. Winter roost site for bald eagles. Watch for golden eagles, red-tailed and ferruginous hawks, and turkey vultures. Lots of ravens and jays. Concentrations of songbirds, on south-facing slopes. Winter range for deer and elk. Watch for chipmunks, ground squirrels, and gray-phase Abert's squirrels.

Ownership: BLM (303-247-4082)
Size: 2,700 acres
Closest Town: Durango
Directions: See map above

123

109 DURANGO FISH HATCHERY

Description: An excellent opportunity to see hatchery operations. Visitors may also feed the fish. Hatchery has a museum, bookstore, interpretive displays, and viewing windows that overlook various hatchery operations.

Viewing Information: Eggs from rainbow, brook, brown, and cutthroat trout are hatched and reared here, then released into the wild to stock lakes and streams. Pools contain fingerlings (fish two to four inches long) and catchables (eight to twelve inches long).

Ownership: CDOW (303-247-4755)
Size: Five acres
Closest Town: Durango
Directions: See map this page

Located downtown on the Animas River, the Durango Fish Hatchery offers visitors the chance to view trout culture practices that are key to maintaing the quality of colorado fisheries. GEOFF TISCHBIEN

110 CHIMNEY ROCK

Description: An archaeological site with ruins of the Chacoan Anasazi culture. From the parking lot, a steep, one-mile trail leads to Chimney Rock, located atop a mesa. Visitors must stay on trails. Semi-arid, pinyon/juniper, and Gambel oak community. Good scenic vistas of the Piedra Valley and Chimney Rock Pinnacles. A fire tower atop the mesa is open to the public. You must have a permit or be on a guided tour to enter the area. Contact the Pagosa Springs office of the Forest Service for tour schedules and permits.

Viewing Information: Good chance of seeing deer and elk. Numerous mammals including porcupines, rabbits, coyotes, chipmunks, and golden-mantled ground squirrels. Short-horned and fence lizards and rattlesnakes in sunny, rocky areas. Wild turkeys, blue grouse, prairie falcons, ravens, crows, and swifts often visible at the site. Many golden and bald eagles may be seen up and down the valley. Tarantulas visible during fall migration.

Ownership: USFS (303-264-2268)
Size: 3,160 acres
Closest Town: Pagosa Springs
Directions: See map this page

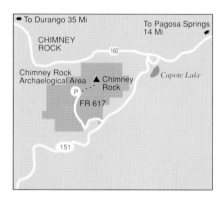

Short-horned lizards have short spines for protection from predators. The lizards are partial to lowland habitats, where their natural coloring matches the local soil and provides additional protection. LAUREN J. LIVO AND STEVE WILCOX

125

50 POPULAR SPECIES
AND WHERE TO FIND THEM

This list does not constitute the only places these species can be viewed. These sites do offer excellent opportunities to view the species, however. Some recommendations made here do not appear in the site descriptions in previous pages. The numbers listed below are site numbers. Check the table of contents to find the correct page for the site you are looking for.

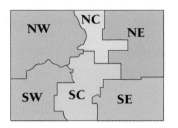

SPECIES	NW SITE	NC SITE	NE SITE	SE SITE	SC SITE	SW SITE
Abert's squirrel		33 39				107 108
American dipper	19	47			85	94
Badger	20	44	51	64		
Bald eagle	22	41 44	53		93	100 104
Beaver	19	31 40	58	62	84 92	105
Black bear		33		63		99 105
Black-billed magpie	10	34		62	87	96
Blue grouse		37			76 80	99 101
Burrowing owl	2 4	44	58	68 72		
Collared lizard				65 71		105 106
Coyote	20	44	61	64 65	79 93	104
Desert bighorn	11					105
Elk	8 16	31 39		63	75 80	98 108
Golden eagle	6	41 44	59	64	80	106 108

SPECIES	NW SITE	NC SITE	NE SITE	SE SITE	SC SITE	SW SITE
Great blue heron		46		68	87	
Great horned owl		30 45			87	
Gray jay	31 37			83	101	
Greater prairie-chicken			55 57			
Lark bunting		44	50			
Least tern				66 70		
Lesser prairie-chicken				74		
Mississippi kite				69		
Moose	23	27			85	
Mountain goat		38				
Mountain lion		33				105 106
Mountain plover			50 51			
Mule deer	2 20 8	35		64	77 89	100
Osprey		30				104
Peregrine falcon	2 3				77 80	105 106
Pika		31 38			85	101
Prairie dog	4	44	51	64 68	80	
Pronghorn	4 21		51 60	64	80	
Red fox		42 43		62 64	78	

SPECIES	NW SITE	NC SITE	NE SITE	SE SITE	SC SITE	SW SITE
River otter	22	31				105
Rocky Mountain bighorn		28 36 47		72	76 82 84	95
Sandhill crane			56		93	
Sage grouse	5 7					97
Sharp-tailed grouse	7		55			
Snowy plover				70	90	
Steller's jay	20	35			83 89	98 106
Trout		34			84	94 96 109
Turkey vulture	20	41	59	64 73		105 106
Weasel				67	76	
Western rattlesnake	4	48 49		65 72		
White-faced ibis					88	
White-tailed deer			55 58	62	77	
White-tailed ptarmigan		31 37 38				101
White pelican		45	52	66	88 90	
Wild turkey			55 58	63 67	77	105
Yellow-bellied marmot	15	31			85	99